# BUSINESS AND LEGAL FORMS

# FOR

# ILLUSTRATORS

## TAD CRAWFORD

ALLWORTH PRESS, NEW YORK

Published by Allworth Press, an imprint of Allworth Communications, Inc., 10 East 23rd Street, New York, NY 10010.

Distributor to the trade in the United States and Canada: North Light Books, an imprint of F&W Publications, Inc., 1507 Dana Avenue, Cincinnati, Ohio 45207. To order additional copies of this book, call toll-free (800) 289-0963.

Book Design by Douglas Design Associates, New York, NY.

Library of Congress Catalog Card Number: 89-80741

ISBN: 0-927629-02-X

# Table of Contents

# The Success Kit

**A**ttaining the knowledge of good business practices and implementing their use is an important step toward success for any professional, including the professional illustrator. The forms contained in this book deal with the most important business transactions that an illustrator is likely to undertake. At the back of the book is an extra copy of each form, perforated on 8 1/2-by-11-inch sheets so that the illustrator can remove them from the book and make copies for use in his or her business. The fact that the forms are designed for use and that they favor the illustrator give them a unique value.

Understanding the business concepts behind the forms is as important as using them. By knowing why a certain provision has been included and what it accomplishes, the illustrator is able to negotiate when faced with someone else's business form. The illustrator knows what is and is not desirable. The negotiation checklists offer a map for the negotiation of any form.

All forms, whether the illustrator's or someone else's, can be changed. Before using these forms, the illustrator should consider reviewing them with his or her attorney. This provides the opportunity to learn whether local or state laws may make it worthwhile to modify any of the provisions. For example, would it be wise to include a provision for arbitration of disputes, or are the local courts speedy and inexpensive, making an arbitration provision unnecessary?

The forms must be filled out, which means that the blanks in each form must be completed. Beyond this, however, the illustrator can always delete or add provisions on any form. Deletions or additions to a form are usually initialed in the margin by both parties. It is also a good practice to have each party initial each page of the contract, except the page on which the parties sign.

The illustrator must ascertain that the person signing the contract has authority to do so. If the illustrator is dealing with a company, the company's name should be included, as well as the name of the individual authorized to sign the contract and the title of that individual. If it isn't clear who will sign or if that person has no title, the words "Authorized Signatory" can be used instead of a title.

If the illustrator will not be meeting with the other party to sign the contract, it would be wise to have that party sign the forms first. After the illustrator gets back the two copies of the form, they can be signed and one copy returned to the other party. As discussed in more detail under letter contracts, this has the advantage of not leaving it up to the other party to decide whether to sign and thus make a binding contract.

If additional provisions that won't fit on the contract forms should be added, simply include a provision stating, "This contract is subject to the provisions of the rider attached hereto and made a part hereof." The rider is simply another piece of paper which would be headed, "Rider to the contract between _____ and _____, dated the ____ day of _____, 19____." The additional provisions are put on this sheet and both parties sign it.

## Contracts and Negotiation

Most of the forms in this book are contracts. A contract is an agreement that creates legally enforceable obligations between two or more parties. In making a contract, each party gives something of value to the other party. This mutual giving of value is called the exchange of consideration. Consideration can take many forms, including the giving of money or an artwork or the promise to create an artwork or pay for an artwork in the future.

Contracts require negotiation. The forms in this book are favorable to the illustrator, so changes may very well be requested. This book's explanation of the use of each form should help the illustrator evaluate changes which either party may want to make in any of the forms. The negotiation checklists should also clarify what changes would be desirable in forms presented to the illustrator.

Keep in mind that negotiation need not be adversarial. Certainly the illustrator and the other party may disagree on some points, but the basic transaction is something that both want. This larger framework of agreement must be kept in mind at all times when negotiating. Of course, the illustrator must also know which points are nonnegotiable and be prepared to walk away from a deal if satisfaction cannot be had on these points.

When both parties have something valuable to offer each other, it should be possible for each side to come away from the negotiation feeling that they have won. Win-win negotiation requires each side to make certain that the basic needs of both are met so that the result is fair. The illustrator cannot negotiate for the other side, but a wise negotiation strategy must allow the other side to meet their vital needs within a larger context that also allows the illustrator to obtain what he or she must have.

It is a necessity to evaluate negotiating goals and strategy before conducting any negotiations. The illustrator should write down what must be achieved and what can be conceded or modified. The illustrator should try to imagine how the shape of the contract will affect the future business relationship with the other party. Will it probably lead to success for both sides and more business or will it fail to achieve what one side or the other desires?

When negotiating, the illustrator should keep written notes close at hand concerning goals and strategy. Notes should be kept on the negotiations too, since many conversations may be necessary before final agreement is reached. At certain points the illustrator should compare what the negotiations are achieving with the original goals. This will help evaluate whether the illustrator is conducting the negotiations according to plan.

Most negotiations are done over the telephone. This makes the telephone a tool to be used wisely. The illustrator should decide when to speak with the other party. Before calling, it is important to review the notes and be familiar with the points to be negotiated. If the illustrator wants the other party to call, the file should be kept close at hand so that there is no question as to where the negotiations stand when the call comes. If the illustrator is unprepared to negotiate when the other side calls, the best course is to call back. Negotiation demands the fullest attention and complete readiness.

## Oral Contracts

Although all the forms in this book are written, the question of oral contracts should be addressed. There are certain contracts that must be written, such as a contract for services that will take more than one year to perform, a contract to transfer an exclusive right of copyright (an exclusive right means that no one else can do what the person receiving that right of copyright can do), or, in many cases, a contract for the sale of goods worth more than $500. So—without delving into the full complexity of this subject—certain contracts can be oral. If the illustrator is faced with a breached oral contract, an attorney should certainly be consulted for advice. The illustrator should not give up simply because the contract was oral.

However, while some oral contracts are valid, a written contract is always best. Even people with the most scrupulous intentions do not always remember exactly what was said or whether a particular point was covered. Disputes, and litigation, are far more likely when a contract is oral rather than written. That likelihood is another reason to make the use of written forms, like those in this book, an integral part of the business practices of any illustrator.

## Letter Contracts

If the illustrator feels that sending a well-drafted form will be daunting to the other party, the more informal approach of a letter, signed by both parties, may be adopted. In this case, the forms in this book will serve as valuable checklists for the content and negotiation of the letter contract. The last paragraph of the letter would read, "If the foregoing meets with your approval, please sign both copies of this letter beneath the words AGREED TO to make this a binding contract between us." At the bottom of the letter would be the words AGREED TO with the name of the other party so he or she can sign. Again, if the other party is a company, the company name, as well as the name of the authorized signatory and that individual's title, would be placed beneath the words AGREED TO. This would appear as follows:

> **AGREED TO:**
> XYZ Corporation
> By_____
> Alice Hall, Vice President

Two copies of this letter are sent to the other party, who is instructed to sign both copies and return one copy for the illustrator to keep. To be cautious, the illustrator can send the letters unsigned and ask the other party to sign and return both copies, at which time the illustrator will sign and return one copy to the other party. This gives the other party an opportunity to review the final draft, but avoids a situation in which the other party may choose to delay signing, thereby preventing the illustrator from offering a similar contract to anyone else because the first contract still may be signed.

For example, if an investment group wanted to wait and see if they could license rights they were contracting to buy in an artwork, they might hold the contract and only sign it after they knew they could sell the license. If the sale of the license did not come through, they might not sign the contract and the deal would be off. The illustrator can avoid this by being the final signatory, by insisting that both parties meet to sign, or by stating in the letter a deadline by which the other party must sign. If such a situation ever arises,

it should be remembered that any offer to enter into a contract can always be revoked up until the time that the contract is actually entered into.

## Standard Provisions

The contracts in this book contain a number of standard provisions, called "boilerplate" by lawyers. These provisions are important, although they will not seem as exciting as the provisions that relate more directly to the illustrator and the artwork. Since these provisions can be used in almost every contract and appear in a number of the contracts in this book, an explanation of each of the provisions is given here.

**Amendment.** Any amendment of this Agreement must be in writing and signed by both parties.

This guarantees that any changes the parties want will be made in writing. It avoids the possibility of one party relying on oral changes to the agreement. Courts will rarely change a written contract based on testimony that there was an oral amendment of the contract.

**Arbitration.** All disputes arising under this Agreement shall be submitted to binding arbitration before _____ in the following location _____ and shall be settled in accordance with the rules of the American Arbitration Association. Judgment upon the arbitration award may be entered in any court having jurisdiction thereof. Notwithstanding the foregoing, either party may refuse to arbitrate when the dispute is for a sum of less than $_____.

Arbitration can offer a quicker and less expensive way to settle disputes than litigation. However, the illustrator would be wise to consult a local attorney and make sure that this is advisable in the jurisdiction where the lawsuit would be likely to take place. The arbitrator could be the American Arbitration Association or some other person or group that both parties trust. The illustrator would also want the arbitration to take place where he or she is located. If small claims court is easy to use in the jurisdiction where the illustrator would have to sue, it might be best to have the right not to arbitrate if the disputed amount is small enough to be brought into the small claims court. In this case, the illustrator would put the maximum amount that can be sued for in small claims court in the space at the end of the paragraph.

**Assignment.** This Agreement shall not be assigned by either party hereto, provided that the Illustrator shall have the right to assign monies due to the Illustrator hereunder.

By not allowing the assignment of a contract, both parties can have greater confidence that the stated transactions will be between the original parties. Of course, a company may be purchased by new owners. If the illustrator only wanted to do business with the people who owned the company when the contract was entered into, change of ownership might be stated as a ground for termination in the contract. On the other hand, money is impersonal and there is no reason why the illustrator should not be able to assign the right to receive money.

**Bankruptcy or Insolvency.** If the Gallery should become insolvent or if a petition in bankruptcy is filed against the Gallery or a Receiver or Trustee is appointed for any of the gallery's assets or property, or if a lien or attachment is obtained against any of the Gallery's assets, this Agreement shall immediately terminate and the Gallery shall return to the Illustrator all of the IlIlustrator's work that is in the Gallery's possession.

This provision seeks to protect the illustrator against creditors of the gallery who might use the illustrator's work or proceeds from that work to satisfy claims they have against the gallery itself.

Because a provision of this kind does not protect the illustrator completely, many states have enacted special consignment laws protecting illustrators and their work. Such a provision should also appear in a publishing or licensing contract, although the bankruptcy law may impede the provision's effectiveness.

**Complete Understanding.** This Agreement constitutes the entire and complete understanding between the parties hereto, and no obligation, undertaking, warranty, representation, or covenant of any kind or nature has been made by either party to the other to induce the making of this Agreement, except as is expressly set forth herein.

This provision is intended to prevent either party from later claiming that any promises or obligations exist except those shown in the written contract. A shorter way to say this is, "This Agreement constitutes the entire understanding between the parties hereto."

**Cumulative Rights.** All rights, remedies, obligations, undertakings, warranties, representations, and covenants contained herein shall be cumulative and none of them shall be in limitation of any other right, remedy, obligation, undertaking, warranty, representation, or covenant of either party.

This means that a benefit or obligation under one provision will not be made less because of a different benefit or obligation under another provision.

**Death or Disability.** In the event of the Illustrator's death, or an incapacity of the Illustrator making completion of the Work impossible, this Agreement shall terminate.

A provision of this kind leaves a great deal to be determined. Will payments already made be kept by the illustrator or the illustrator's estate? And who will own the work at whatever stage of completion has been reached? These issues should be resolved when the contract is negotiated.

**Force Majeure.** If either party hereto is unable to perform any of its obligations hereunder by reason of fire or other casualty, strike, act or order of a public authority, act of God, or other cause beyond the control of such party, then such party shall be excused from such performance during the pendancy of such cause. In the event such inability to perform shall continue longer than ____ days, either party may terminate this Agreement by giving written notice to the other party.

This provision covers events beyond the control of the parties, such as a tidal wave or a war. Certainly the time to perform the contract should be extended in such an event. There may be an issue as to how long an extension should be allowed. Also, if work has commenced and some payments have been made, the contract should cover what happens in the event of termination. Must the payments be returned? And who owns the partially completed work?

**Governing Law.** This Agreement shall be governed by the laws of the State of_____.

Usually the illustrator would want the laws of his or her own state to govern the agreement. However, laws vary from state to state. A number of states have enacted laws favoring illustrators, especially in the area of consignments of art to a gallery. If the illustrator's own state lacks this law, it might be preferable to have a gallery contract governed by the law of a different state that has such a consignment law. To find out if a state has such a law, refer to the volunteer lawyers for the arts section of this text, following the discussion of standard provisions.

**Indemnify and Hold Harmless.** The Purchaser agrees to indemnify and hold harmless the Illustrator from any and all claims, demands, payments, expenses, legal fees, or other costs in relation to obligations for materials or services incurred by the Purchaser.

This provision protects one party against damaging actions that may have been taken by the other party. Often, one party will warrant that something is true and then indemnify and hold the other party harmless in the event that it is not true. See the discussion of "Warranties" later in this section. A warranty is usually accompanied by an indemnity clause.

**Liquidated Damages.** In the event of the failure of XYZ Corporation to deliver by the due date, the agreed upon damages shall be $ ____ for each day after the due date until delivery takes place, provided the amount of damages shall not exceed $____.

Liquidated damages are an attempt to anticipate in the contract what damages will be caused by a breach of the contract. Such liquidated damages must be reasonable. If they are not, they will be considered a penalty and held to be unenforceable.

**Modification.** This Agreement cannot be changed, modified, or discharged, in whole or in part, except by an instrument in writing, signed by the party against whom enforcement of any change, modification, or discharge is sought.

This requires that a change in the contract must be written and signed by the party against whom the change will be enforced. It should be compared with the provision for amendments that requires any modification to be in writing and signed by both parties. At the least, however, this provision explicitly avoids the claim that an oral modification has been made of a written contract.

Almost invariably, courts will give greater weight to a written document than to testimony about oral agreements.

**Notices and Changes of Address.** All notices shall be sent to the Illustrator at the following address:_____
and to the Purchaser at the following address:
_____. Each party shall be given written notification of any change of address prior to the date of said change.

Contracts often require the giving of notice. This provision facilitates giving notice by providing correct addresses and requiring notification of any change of address.

**Successors and Assigns.** This Agreement shall be binding upon and inure to the benefit of the parties hereto and their respective heirs, executors, administrators, successors, and assigns.

This makes the contract binding on anyone who takes the place of one of the parties, whether due to death or simply to an assignment of the contract. Note that the standard provision on assignment in fact does not allow assignment, but that provision could always be modified in the original contract or by a later written, signed amendment to the contract.

**Time.** Time is of the essence.

This requires both parties to perform to the exact time commitments they have made or be in breach of the contract. It is not a wise provision for the illustrator to agree to, since being a few days late in performance could cause the loss of benefits under the contract.

**Waivers.** No waiver by either party of any of the terms or conditions of this Agreement shall be deemed or construed to be a waiver of such term or condition for the future, or of any subsequent breach thereof.

This means that if one party waives a right under the contract, such as the right to approve the sketch on the first of a series of illustrations, that party has not waived the right forever and can demand that the other party perform at the next opportunity. So the client would still have the right to approve sketches for the rest of the illustrations in the series. And if the client breached the contract in some other way, such as not paying money due, the fact that the illustrator allowed this once would not prevent the illustrator from suing for such a breach in the future.

**Warranties.** The Illustrator hereby warrants that he or she is the sole creator of the Work and owns all rights granted under this Agreement.

A warranty is something the other party can rely on to be true. If the illustrator states a fact that is a basic reason for the other party's entry into the contract, then that fact is a warranty and must be true. For example, the illustrator might state that he or she is the sole creator of certain artwork, owns the copyright therein, and has not infringed anyone else's copyright in creating the work. If this were not true, the illustrator would be liable for damages caused to the other party under the indemnity clause of the contract.

## Volunteer Lawyers for the Arts

There are now volunteer lawyers for the arts across the nation. These groups provide free assistance to illustrators below certain income levels and can be a valuable source of information. If, for example, it is not clear whether a certain law to benefit illustrators (such as a gallery consignment law) has been enacted in a state, the illustrator should be able to find out by calling the closest volunteer lawyers for the arts group. To find the location of that group, one of the groups listed here can be contacted:

**California:** California Lawyers for the Arts, Fort Mason Center, Building C, Room 255, San Francisco, California 94123, (415) 775-7200; and 315 West 9th Street, Suite 1101, Los Angeles, California 90015, (213) 623-8811.

**Illinois:** Lawyers for the Creative Arts, 213 West Institute Place, Suite 411, Chicago, Illinois 60610, (312) 944-2787.

**New York:** Volunteer Lawyers for the Arts, 1285 Avenue of the Americas, New York, New York 10019, (212) 977-9270.

A helpful handbook covering all the legal issues which illustrators face is *Legal Guide for the Visual Artist* by Tad Crawford (Allworth Press, distributed by North Light Books). Another good resource is *Selling Your Graphic Design and Illustration* by Tad Crawford and Arie Kopelman (St. Martin's Press).

Having reviewed the basics of dealing with business and legal forms, the next step is to move on to the forms themselves and the negotiation checklists that will make the forms most useful.

## Using the Negotiation Checklists

These checklists focus on the key points for negotiation. When a point is covered in the contract already, the appropriate paragraph is indicated in the checklist. These checklists are also valuable to use when reviewing a form given to the illustrator by someone else.

If the illustrator will provide the form, the boxes can be checked to be certain all important points are covered. If the illustrator is reviewing someone else's form, checking the boxes will show which points are covered and which points may have to be added. By using the paragraph numbers in the checklist, the other party's provision can be quickly compared with a provision that would favor the illustrator. Each checklist for a contract concludes with the suggestion that the standard provisions be reviewed to see if any

should be added to those the form provides.

Of course, the illustrator does not have to include every point on the checklist in a contract, but being aware of these points will be helpful. After the checklists, the exact wording is provided for some of the more important provisions that might be added to the form. Starting with Form 1, the explanations go through each of the forms in sequence.

# Estimate

**F**orm 1 (Estimate), Form 2 (Confirmation of Assignment), and Form 3 (Invoice) are closely related. In a perfect world, the client would describe the assignment and would then receive the estimate from the illustrator. After agreeing to the specifications and terms of the estimate, both parties would sign the confirmation of assignment, which repeats the nearly identical specifications and terms. When the assignment has been completed, the invoice would be given to the client. It too would conform to the specifications and terms of the estimate and the confirmation of assignment.

As we know, illustrations are frequently sold without proper documentation. If the client calls for a rush job, the illustrator wants to do the illustrations by the deadline and may skip the paperwork. If the client has sent a purchase order, the illustrator may feel that the purchase order is sufficient documentation or be concerned about contradicting its terms in the confirmation of assignment.

The truth is that inadequate documentation is a disservice to the client as well as the illustrator. There are a number of issues which the parties must resolve. The client as well as the illustrator wants to know the rights being transferred. The rights must be adequate for the client's intended use of the art. The nature of the art to be done, the due dates for sketches and finishes, and the fee to be paid are important to have in writing, since a talk on the phone can more easily be given different interpretations by the parties. The client as well as the illustrator wants to know if there will be reimbursement for expenses, how payment will be made, what happens in the event of cancellation, and how revisions will be handled. Some of the other provisions in the estimate include authorship credit, copyright notice, releases, ownership of the original art, and arbitration.

The estimate, confirmation of assignment, and invoice exist for different reasons. If the illustra-

tor knew that a confirmation of assignment would be signed for every job, the estimate and invoice could be far briefer. The estimate would merely describe the assignment, give a fee, and state that the assignment will be governed by a confirmation of assignment which must be signed by both parties before work commences. If there were a confirmation of assignment signed by both parties, the invoice would show an amount due and state that it was being issued in conformity with the terms of the confirmation of assignment.

In fact, the illustrator cannot be certain that a confirmation of assignment will be signed by the client or, if it is signed, when it will be signed. For that reason, and the possibility that the client may provide a purchase order or check with a restrictive legend, it is wise to have the specifications and terms on each document that the illustrator provides to the client.

The illustrator should resolve conflicts between his or her forms and those of the client immediately. If the estimate is given, work commences, and no other forms are exchanged until the invoice is sent, the estimate will probably be found either to be a contract or, at least, to be evidence of an oral contract. On the other hand, if the estimate conflicts with the client's purchase order, it will be very difficult to know in retrospect which terms the parties agreed to on those points where the forms differ. So, the illustrator should point out and resolve such issues without delay. Or if the illustrator has not given an estimate or confirmation of assignment, but disagrees with the terms of a purchase order, reliance on the invoice to resolve these issues would not be wise. It is unlikely, for example, that an invoice alone can govern the terms of a transaction, simply because it is given to the client after the transaction has been concluded.

The estimate, like any of the forms in this book, could be simplified as either a form or a letter including only the terms which the illustrator feels are most important. Form 1 seeks to resolve issues which frequently arise and to protect the illustrator. Certainly, it is better to raise such issues at the outset of the assignment, rather than disagree later. Such disagreements are far more likely to cause the loss of clients than is a frank discussion of the terms before any work has been done.

With slight modifications in Forms 1, 2, and 3, the illustrator may choose to develop an estimate/confirmation-of-assignment/invoice form. A box would be checked to indicate which purpose the form is to be used for and it would be filled in appropriately. In this book, however, the forms are separate, since each has a different purpose and is intended for use at a different time in the relationship with the client.

Because the estimate, confirmation of assignment, and invoice are closely related, the negotiation checklists are very similar. For that reason, the negotiation checklist for Form 1 covers the points which should appear in a short-form estimate and assumes that Form 2 will be signed before work commences. If Form 1 is to be used, and especially if Form 1 is likely to be the only form used, then the negotiation checklist for Form 2 must be reviewed by the illustrator. The negotiation checklist for Form 2 should also be used to review the purchase order or contract form offered by a client.

## Filling in the Form

The illustrator should provide his or her letterhead, then fill in the date, the client's name and address, the illustrator's number for the job, and the number of any purchase order given by the client. In Paragraph 1 the work should be described in detail. In Paragraph 2, specify how many days it will take to go from starting work to sketches and from approval of sketches to finished art. In Paragraph 3 give the limitations on the rights granted. In Paragraph 5 state the fee. In Paragraph 7 specify the types of expenses to be reimbursed by the client and the amount of any advance to be paid against expenses. In Paragraph 8 give a monthly interest rate. Fill in Paragraph 9 if advances on the fee are to be paid. Check the boxes in Paragraphs 11 and 12 to indicate whether copyright notice or authorship credit will be given in the name of the illustrator. State in Paragraph 13 the percentages of the total fee that will be paid for cancellation at various stages of work. In Paragraph 14 fill in a value for the original art. In Paragraph 16 specify who will arbitrate disputes, where this will be done, and the maximum amount which can be sued for in small claims court. In Paragraph 17 give the state whose laws will govern the contract. The illustrator can then sign the estimate. If the client agrees to the estimate and it will not be possible to obtain a signed confirmation of assignment before work begins, the words "AGREED TO" can be added and the client can sign the estimate.

## Negotiation Checklist

❏ State that a confirmation of assignment form is to be signed before the commencement of work. (Preamble)

❏ Describe the assignment in as much detail as possible, attaching another sheet to the contract if necessary (in which case the line for Subject Matter would refer to the attached sheet). (Paragraph 1)

❏ Give a due date for sketches, which can be expressed as a number of days after client's approval for illustrator to start work. (Paragraph 2)

❏ If the client is to provide reference materials, the due date should be expressed as a number of days after the illustrator's receipt of these materials. (Paragraph 2)

❑ The due date for finishes should be expressed as a number of days after the client's approval of sketches. (Paragraph 2)

❑ Limit the grant of rights and state that the transfer of rights takes place when the illustrator is paid in full. (Paragraph 3)

❑ Specify whether the client's use of the art will be exclusive or nonexclusive. (Paragraph 3)

❑ All rights not granted to the client should be reserved to the illustrator, including rights in sketches and any other preliminary materials. (Paragraph 4)

❑ The fee must be specified, including the obligation of the client to pay sales taxes. (Paragraph 5)

❑ Any expenses, including markups, which the client will reimburse to the illustrator should be specified to avoid misunderstandings. (Paragraph 7)

❑ If expenses will be significant, provide for an advance against expenses. (Paragraph 7)

❑ Require payment within thirty days of delivery of the finished art. (Paragraph 8)

❑ Specify advances to be paid against the fee, either on signing the contract, on approval of sketches, or at both times. A schedule of payments is especially important for an extensive job. (Paragraph 9)

❑ State whether the illustrator's copyright notice will appear with the art. (Paragraph 11)

❑ State whether the illustrator will receive name credit with the art. (Paragraph 12)

❑ Fees for cancellation at different stages of the assignment must be specified, plus payment of any expenses incurred. (Paragraph 13)

❑ State that the illustrator shall own all rights in the work in the event of cancellation. (Paragraph 13)

❑ Specify a time for payment of cancellation fees, such as within thirty days of client's stopping work or the delivery of finished art, whichever occurs first. (Paragraph 13)

❑ Require the client to return the art within thirty days after use. (Paragraph 14)

❑ Review the standard provisions in the introductory pages and compare to Paragraph 17.

❑ Review the negotiation checklist for Form 2, especially if Form 1 is going to be used without Form 2 or if the illustrator is reviewing a purchase order or contract provided by the client.

< Illustrator's Letterhead >

# Estimate

Client _____ Date _____

Address _____

Client Purchase Order Number _____ Job Number _____

This Estimate is based on the specifications and terms which follow. If the Client confirms that the Illustrator should proceed with the assignment based on this Estimate, it is understood that the assignment shall be subject to the terms shown on this Estimate and that Client shall sign a Confirmation of Assignment form incorporating the same specifications and terms. If the assignment proceeds without a Confirmation of Assignment being signed by both parties, the assignment shall be governed by the terms and conditions contained in this Estimate.

1. **Description**. The Illustrator shall create the Work in accordance with the following specifications:

   Subject matter _____

   Number of illustrations in color _____

   Number of illustrations in black and white _____

   Size of illustrations _____

   Medium for illustrations _____

   Other specifications _____

2. **Due Date**. Sketches shall be delivered within _____ days after either the Client's authorization to commence work or, if the Client is to provide reference, layouts, or specifications, after the Client has provided same to the Illustrator, whichever occurs later. Finished art shall be delivered _____ days after the approval of sketches by the Client.

3. **Grant of Rights**. Upon receipt of full payment, the Illustrator shall grant to the Client the following rights in the finished art:

   For use as _____

   For the product or publication named _____

   In the following territory _____

   For the following time period _____

   Other limitations _____

   With respect to the usage shown above, the Client shall have ❏ exclusive ❏ nonexclusive rights.

   If the finished art is for use as a contribution to a magazine, the grant of rights shall be first North American serial rights only unless specified to the contrary above.

4. **Reservation of Rights.** All rights not expressly granted shall be reserved to the Illustrator, including but not limited to all rights in sketches, comps, or other preliminary materials.

5. **Fee**. Client shall pay the following purchase price: $_____ for the usage rights granted. Client shall also pay sales tax, if required.

6. **Additional Usage.** If Client wishes to make any additional uses of the Work, Client shall seek permission from the Illustrator and pay an additional fee to be agreed upon.

7. **Expenses.** Client shall reimburse the Illustrator for the following expenses: ❏ Messenger ❏ Models ❏ Props ❏ Travel ❏ Telephone ❏ Other _____ At the time of signing the Confirmation of Assignment or the commencement of work, whichever is first, Client shall pay Illustrator $_____ as a nonrefundable advance against expenses. If the advance exceeds expenses incurred, the credit balance shall be used to reduce the fee payable, or, if the fee has been fully paid, shall be reimbursed to Client.

8. **Payment.** Client shall pay the Illustrator within thirty days of the date of Illustrator's billing, which shall be dated as of the date of delivery of the finished art. In the event that work is postponed at the request of the Client, the Illustrator shall have the right to bill pro rata for work completed through the date of that request, while reserving all other rights. Overdue payments shall be subject to interest charges of _____ percent monthly.

9. **Advances.** At the time of signing the Confirmation of Assignment or the commencement of work, whichever is first, Client shall pay Illustrator _____ percent of the fee as an advance against the total fee. Upon approval of sketches Client shall pay Illustrator _____ percent of the fee as an advance against the total fee.

10. **Revisions.** The Illustrator shall be given the first opportunity to make any revisions requested by the Client. If the revisions are not due to any fault on the part of the Illustrator, an additional fee shall be charged. If the Illustrator objects to any revisions to be made by the Client, the Illustrator shall have the right to have his or her name removed from the published Work.

11. **Copyright Notice.** Copyright notice in the name of the Illustrator ❑ shall ❑ shall not accompany the Work when it is reproduced.

12. **Authorship Credit.** Authorship credit in the name of the Illustrator ❑ shall ❑ shall not accompany the Work when it is reproduced. If the finished art is used as a contribution to a magazine or for a book, authorship credit shall be given unless specified to the contrary in the preceding sentence.

13. **Cancellation.** In the event of cancellation by the Client, the following cancellation payment shall be paid by the Client: **(A)** Cancellation prior to the finished art being turned in: _____ percent of fee; **(B)** Cancellation due to finished art being unsatisfactory: _____ percent of fee; and **(C)** Cancellation for any other reason after the finished art is turned in: _____ percent of fee. In the event of cancellation, the Client shall also pay any expenses incurred by the Illustrator and the Illustrator shall own all rights in the Work. The billing upon cancellation shall be payable within thirty days of the Client's notification to stop work or the delivery of the finished art, whichever occurs sooner.

14. **Ownership and Return of Artwork.** The ownership of original artwork, including sketches and any other materials created in the process of making the finished art, shall remain with the Illustrator. All such artwork shall be returned to the Illustrator by bonded messenger, air freight, or registered mail within thirty days of the Client's completing its use of the artwork. Based on the specifications for the Work, a reasonable value for the original, finished art is $_____.

15. **Permissions and Releases.** The Client shall indemnify and hold harmless the Illustrator against any and all claims, costs, and expenses, including attorney's fees, due to materials included in the work at the request of the Client for which no copyright permission or privacy release was requested or uses which exceed the uses allowed pursuant to a permission or release.

16. **Arbitration.** All disputes shall be submitted to binding arbitration before _____ in the following location _____ and settled in accordance with the rules of the American Arbitration Association. Judgment upon the arbitration award may be entered in any court having jurisdiction thereof. Disputes in which the amount at issue is less than $_____ shall not be subject to this arbitration provision.

17. **Miscellany.** If the Client authorizes the Illustrator to commence work, the terms of this Estimate Form shall be binding upon the parties, their heirs, successors, assigns, and personal representatives; the Estimate Form constitutes the entire understanding between the parties; its terms can be modified only by an instrument in writing signed by both parties, except that the Client may authorize expenses and revisions orally; a waiver of a breach of any of its provisions shall not be construed as a continuing waiver of other breaches of the same or other provisions hereof; and the relationship between the Client and Illustrator shall be governed by the laws of the State of _____.

Illustrator _____

# Confirmation of Assignment

Form 2, the Confirmation of Assignment, follows Form 1, the Estimate, almost exactly. Ideally, the client will review the estimate and request whatever changes are necessary. Then both client and illustrator will sign Form 2 to make a binding contract. If Form 1 has not been given to the client, or if an estimate has been used which only gives limited information such as a project description and a price, then it is even more important to use Form 2. By signing Form 2 before the commencement of the assignment, the parties resolve many of the issues likely to cause disputes. Since the goal with any client is to create a long-term relationship, the avoidance of needless disputes is a very positive step. If the client requests changes in Form 2, the illustrator can certainly make revisions. Nonetheless, the agreement between the parties will be clear, which promotes creating the best art and a long-term business relationship.

## Filling in the Form

Fill in the date and the names and addresses for the client and the illustrator. In Paragraph 1 describe the assignment in detail, attaching an additional sheet to the form if needed. Give the illustrator's number for the job and the number of any purchase order given by the client. In Paragraph 2, specify how many days it will take to go from starting work to sketches and from approval of sketches to finished art. In Paragraph 3 give the limitations on the rights granted and specify whether the client's rights are exclusive or nonexclusive. In Paragraph 5 state the fee. In Paragraph 7 specify the types of expenses to be reimbursed by the client and the amount of any advance to be paid against expenses. In Paragraph 8 give a monthly interest rate for late payments. Fill in Paragraph 9 if advances on the fee are to be paid. Check the boxes in Paragraphs 11 and 12 to indicate whether copyright notice or authorship credit will be given in the name of the illustrator. In Paragraph 13 state the percentages of the total fee that will be paid for cancellation at various stages of work. In Paragraph 14 fill in a value for the original art. In Paragraph 16 specify who will arbitrate disputes, where this will be done, and give the maximum amount which can be sued for in small claims court. In Paragraph 17 give the state whose laws will govern the contract. Both parties should then sign the contract.

## Negotiation Checklist

❑ Describe the assignment in as much detail as possible, attaching another sheet to the contract if necessary (in which case the line for Subject Matter would refer to the attached sheet). (Paragraph 1)

❑ Give a due date for sketches, which can be expressed as a number of days after client's approval for illustrator to start work. (Paragraph 2)

❑ If the client is to provide reference materials, the due date should be expressed as a number of days after the illustrator's receipt of these materials. (Paragraph 2)

❑ The due date for finishes should be expressed as a number of days after the client's approval of sketches. (Paragraph 2)

❑ Time should not be of the essence.

❑ State that illness or other delays beyond the control of the illustrator will extend the due date, but only up to a limited number of days.

❑ State that the grant of rights takes place when the illustrator is paid in full. (Paragraph 3)

❑ Limit the grant of rights to the finished art, so that rights in sketches or other work products are not transferred. (Paragraph 3)

❑ Specify whether the client's use of the art will be exclusive or nonexclusive. (Paragraph 3)

❑ Limit the exclusivity to the particular use the client will make of the art, such as for a book jacket, point of purchase ad, or direct mail brochure. This leaves the illustrator free to resell the art for other uses. (Paragraph 3)

❑ Name the product or publication on which the illustration will appear. (Paragraph 3)

❑ Give a geographic limitation, such as local, regional, the United States, North America, and so on. (Paragraph 3)

❑ Limit the time period of use. (Paragraph 3)

❑ Other limitations might include the number of uses. One-time use, for example, means that the illustration cannot be given other uses. Or the use might be restricted to one form of a book, such as hardcover, which would mean that the illustrator would receive reuse fees for subsequent use in paperback. Or the use might be for only one printing of a book, so a second printing would require a reuse fee. It might also specify the size of the illustration's usage, such as a spot as opposed to a full page. The concept behind such limitations is that fees are based on the type and number of usages. (Paragraph 3)

❑ For contributions to magazines, the sale of first North American serial rights is common. This gives the magazine the right to be the first magazine to make a one-time use of the illustration in North America. This could be limited to first United States serial rights. If no agreement about rights is made for a magazine contribution, the copyright law provides that the magazine has a nonexclusive right to use the illustration as many times as it wishes in issues of the magazine but can make no other uses. (Paragraph 3)

❑ All rights not granted to the client should be reserved to the illustrator, including rights in sketches and any other preliminary materials. (Paragraph 4)

❑ If the client insists on all rights or work for hire, offer instead a provision stating, "Illustrator shall not permit any uses of the art which compete with or impair the use of the art by the Client." If necessary to reassure the Client, this might also state, "The Illustrator shall submit any proposed uses to the Client for approval, which shall not be unreasonably withheld."

❑ Many illustrators refuse to do work for hire, since the client becomes the author under the copyright law. The illustrator can point out to the client that work for hire devalues and can damage the creative process.

❑ In the face of a demand for all rights or work for hire, advise the client that fees are based on rights of usage. The fee for all rights or work for hire should be substantially higher than for limited usage.

❑ If the work is highly specific to one client, selling all rights for a higher fee would be more acceptable than for a work likely to have resale value for the illustrator.

❑ If the client demands a "buyout," find out how the client defines this. It can mean the purchase of all rights in the copyright; it may be work for hire; and it may or may not involve purchasing the physical art as well as the copyright.

❑ Do not allow the client to assign usage rights without the consent of the illustrator, since the client may benefit from reuse fees that more appropriately belong to the illustrator.

❑ The fee must be specified. (Paragraph 5)

❑ The obligation of the client to pay sales tax should be included. Many states charge sales tax on the transfer if a physical object is sold to or altered by the client, while sales of reproduction rights (where the illustrator receives the art back without changes) would not be subject to sales tax. However, the laws vary widely from state to state. The illustrator must check the law in his or her state, since the failure to collect and pay sales tax can result in substantial liability. (Paragraph 5)

❑ If additional usage rights are sought by the client, additional fees should be agreed upon and paid. (Paragraph 6)

❑ If it is likely that a certain type of additional usage will be made, the amount of the reuse fee can be specified. Or the reuse fee can be expressed as a percentage of the original fee.

❑ Any expenses which the client will reimburse to the illustrator should be specified to avoid misunderstandings. (Paragraph 7)

❑ If expenses are going to be marked up, this should be stated. The rationale for marking up expenses is that the expenditure ties up the illustrator's funds until he or she receives reimbursement and makes extra paperwork for the illustrator. If expenses are modest, however, most illustrators cover them in the fee.

❑ If expenses will be significant, provide for an advance against expenses. (Paragraph 7)

❑ Specify that any advance against expenses is nonrefundable unless, of course, the expenses are not incurred. (Paragraph 7)

❑ If the client insists on a binding budget for expenses, provide for some flexibility, such as a 10 percent variance, or for client's approval of expense items which exceed the variance.

❑ Require payment within thirty days of delivery of the finished art. (Paragraph 8)

❑ Avoid a usurious interest rate. (Paragraph 8)

❑ Deal with the issue of payment for work-in-progress that is postponed but not cancelled, perhaps by pro rata billing. (Paragraph 8)

❑ Specify advances to be paid against the fee, either on signing the contract, on approval of sketches, or at both times. A schedule of payments is especially important for an extensive job. (Paragraph 9)

❑ State that any advances against the fee are nonrefundable. This is not included in Paragraph 9 because of the interplay with the cancellation provision in Paragraph 13.

❑ Revisions can be a problem. Certainly the illustrator should be given the first opportunity to make revisions. (Paragraph 10)

❑ If revisions are the fault of the illustrator, no additional fee should be charged. However, if the client changes the nature of the assignment, additional fees must be charged for revisions. (Paragraph 10)

❑ Consider limiting the amount of time the illustrator must spend on revisions, whether or not the revisions are the illustrator's fault.

❏ If the client ultimately has revisions done by someone else, the illustrator should reserve the right to have his or her name removed from the art. (Paragraph 10)

❏ With respect to revisions or the assignment itself, additional charges might be specified for work which must be rushed and requires unusual hours or other stresses.

❏ Any revisions or changes in the assignment should be documented in writing, if possible, since there may be a question later as to whether the changes were approved and whether they came within the initial description of the project. (Paragraphs 10 and 17)

❏ State whether copyright notice in the illustrator's name be required to appear with the art. (Paragraph 11)

❏ State whether the illustrator will receive name credit with the art. (Paragraph 12)

❏ For editorial work, require authorship credit as the general rule. One of the values of editorial work is its promotional impact, so name credit is important.

❏ Specify that the type size for authorship credit shall be no smaller than the type around the illustration and that the credit must be adjacent to the illustration.

❏ If authorship credit should be given but is omitted, require payment of an additional fee.

❏ Fees for cancellation at different stages of the assignment must be specified. This very much depends on the work patterns of the illustrator. For example, sketches may be very rough or they may be nearly finished art. Cancella-

tion fees might be 50 percent of the total fee for rejection of sketches or for unsatisfactory finished art, but 100 percent for cancellation for any other reason once art has been turned in. The illustrator must also be reimbursed for expenses incurred. (Paragraph 13)

❏ State that the illustrator shall own all rights in the work in the event of cancellation. (Paragraph 13)

❏ Specify a time for payment of cancellation fees, such as within thirty days of client's stopping work or of the delivery of finished art, whichever comes first. (Paragraph 13)

❏ Never work on speculation (a situation in which no fees will be paid in the event of cancellation or a failure to use the work).

❏ Specify that if the illustration is not published within a certain time period, the rights shall revert to the illustrator. This would avoid, for example, a situation in which a magazine purchases first North American serial rights but never uses the illustration. Since the illustrator cannot make use of the illustration until after publication, the failure to publish would be damaging to the illustrator.

❏ State that the illustrator owns the finished art and any preliminary sketches or materials. (Paragraph 14)

❏ If preliminary sketches are published, the fee should increase to the price for finished art.

❏ If physical art is to be sold, a separate price should be specified.

❏ Require the client to return the art within thirty days after use. (Paragraph 14)

❏ Specify a safe method for the return of the art. (Paragraph 14)

❏ Indicate a value for the art, which can serve as a basis for damages if the client does not take reasonable care of it.

❏ Raise the standard of care which the client must give the art, such as making the client strictly liable for loss or damage to the art while it is in the client's possession or even in transit.

❏ Require the client to insure the art at the value specified for it.

❏ Try not to give a warranty and indemnity provision, in which the illustrator states the work is not a copyright infringement and not libelous and agrees to pay for the client's damages and attorney's fees if this is not true (falsity would be a breach of warranty).

❏ If there is a warranty and indemnity provision, try to be covered under any publisher's liability insurance policy owned by the client and ask the client to cover the deductible.

❏ If the client insists on a warranty and indemnity provision, seek to limit the illustrator's liability to a specified amount. For example, liability might be limited to the amount of the fee for the assignment.

❏ Require the client to indemnify the illustrator if the client wants certain materials to be included in the illustration but does not request that the illustrator obtain needed copyright permissions or privacy releases or uses the illustration in a way that exceeds the use allowed by the permissions or releases. (Paragraph 15)

❏ Provide for arbitration, except for amounts which can be sued for in small claims court. (Paragraph 16)

❏ Review the standard provisions in the introductory pages and compare to Paragraph 17.

# Confirmation of Assignment

AGREEMENT as of the _____ day of _____, 19 _____, between _____,
(hereinafter referred to as the "Client"), located at _____,
and _____ (hereinafter referred to as the "Illustrator"),
located at _____, with
respect to the creation of certain illustrations (hereinafter referred to as the "Work").

WHEREAS, Illustrator is a professional illustrator of good standing;

WHEREAS, Client wishes the Illustrator to create certain Work described more fully herein; and

WHEREAS, Illustrator wishes to create such Work;

NOW, THEREFORE, in consideration of the foregoing premises and the mutual covenants hereinafter set forth and other valuable considerations, the parties hereto agree as follows:

1.  **Description.** The Illustrator agrees to create the Work in accordance with the following specifications:

    Subject matter _____

    Number of illustrations in color _____

    Number of illustrations in black and white _____

    Size of illustrations _____

    Medium for illustrations _____

    Other specifications _____

    Client purchase order number _____ Job number _____

2.  **Due Date.** The Illustrator agrees to deliver sketches within _____ days after the later of the signing of this Agreement or, if the Client is to provide reference, layouts, or specifications, after the Client has provided same to the Illustrator. Finished art shall be delivered _____ days after the approval of sketches by the Client.

3.  **Grant of Rights.** Upon receipt of full payment, the Illustrator grants to the Client the following rights in the finished art:

    For use as _____

    For the product or publication named _____

    In the following territory _____

    For the following time period _____

    Other limitations _____

    With respect to the usage shown above, the Client shall have ❏ exclusive ❏ nonexclusive rights.

    If the finished art is for use as a contribution to a magazine, the grant of rights shall be for first North American serial rights only unless specified to the contrary above.

4.  **Reservation of Rights.** All rights not expressly granted hereunder are reserved to the Illustrator, including but not limited to all rights in sketches, comps, or other preliminary materials.

5.  **Fee.** Client agrees to pay the following purchase price: $_____ for the usage rights granted. Client agrees to pay sales tax, if required.

6.  **Additional Usage.** If Client wishes to make any additional uses of the Work, Client agrees to seek permission from the Illustrator and make such payments as are agreed to between the parties at that time.

7.  **Expenses.** Client agrees to reimburse the Illustrator for the following expenses: ❏ Messengers ❏ Models ❏ Props ❏ Travel ❏ Telephone ❏ Other _____

    At the time of signing this Agreement, Client shall pay Illustrator $_____ as a nonrefundable advance against expenses. If the advance exceeds expenses incurred, the credit balance shall be used to reduce the fee payable or, if the fee has been fully paid, shall be reimbursed to Client.

8. **Payment.** Client agrees to pay the Illustrator within thirty days of the date of Illustrator's billing, which shall be dated as of the date of delivery of the finished art. In the event that work is postponed at the request of the Client, the Illustrator shall have the right to bill pro rata for work completed through the date of that request, while reserving all other rights under this Agreement. Overdue payments shall be subject to interest charges of _____ percent monthly.

9. **Advances.** At the time of signing this Agreement, Client shall pay Illustrator ____ percent of the fee as an advance against the total fee. Upon approval of sketches Client shall pay Illustrator ____ percent of the fee as an advance against the total fee.

10. **Revisions.** The Illustrator shall be given the first opportunity to make any revisions requested by the Client. If the revisions are not due to any fault on the part of the Illustrator, an additional fee shall be charged. If the Illustrator objects to any revisions to be made by the Client, the Illustrator shall have the right to have his or her name removed from the published Work.

11. **Copyright Notice.** Copyright notice in the Illustrator's name ❏ shall ❏ shall not be published with the Work.

12. **Authorship Credit.** Authorship credit in the name of the Illustrator ❏ shall ❏ shall not accompany the Work when it is reproduced. If the finished art is used as a contribution to a magazine or for a book, authorship credit shall be given unless specified to the contrary in the preceding sentence.

13. **Cancellation.** In the event of cancellation by the Client, the following cancellation payment shall be paid by the Client: **(A)** Cancellation prior to the finished art being turned in: ____% of fee; **(B)** Cancellation due to finished art being unsatisfactory: ____% of fee; and **(C)** Cancellation for any other reason after the finished art is turned in: ____% of fee. In the event of cancellation, the Client shall also pay any expenses incurred by the Illustrator and the Illustrator shall own all rights in the Work. The billing upon cancellation shall be payable within thirty days of the Client's notification to stop work or the delivery of the finished art, whichever occurs sooner.

14. **Ownership and Return of Artwork.** The ownership of original artwork, including sketches and any other materials created in the process of making the finished art, shall remain with the Illustrator. All such artwork shall be returned to the Illustrator by bonded messenger, air freight, or registered mail within thirty days of the Client's completing its use of the artwork. The parties agree that the value of the original, finished art is $_____.

15. **Permissions and Releases.** The Client agrees to indemnify and hold harmless the Illustrator against any and all claims, costs, and expenses, including attorney's fees, due to materials included in the Work at the request of the Client for which no copyright permission or privacy release was requested or uses which exceed the uses allowed pursuant to a permission or release.

16. **Arbitration.** All disputes arising under this Agreement shall be submitted to binding arbitration before _____ in the following location _____ and settled in accordance with the rules of the American Arbitration Association. Judgment upon the arbitration award may be entered in any court having jurisdiction thereof. Disputes in which the amount at issue is less than $_____ shall not be subject to this arbitration provision.

17. **Miscellany.** This Agreement shall be binding upon the parties hereto, their heirs, successors, assigns, and personal representatives. This Agreement constitutes the entire understanding between the parties. Its terms can be modified only by an instrument in writing signed by both parties, except that the Client may authorize expenses or revisions orally. A waiver of a breach of any of the provisions of this Agreement shall not be construed as a continuing waiver of other breaches of the same or other provisions hereof. This Agreement shall be governed by the laws of the State of _____.

IN WITNESS WHEREOF, the parties hereto have signed this Agreement as of the date first set forth above.

Illustrator _____     Client _____
                                                          Company Name

                                                 By _____
                                                          Authorized Signatory, Title

# Invoice

**F**orm 3, the Invoice, is rendered to the client when the assignment is completed. It can be handed over with the final art or after the final art has been approved. If Form 2, the Confirmation of Assignment, has already been signed by the client, then the invoice can be quite simple. It need only supply the fee, any expenses to be reimbursed, plus any sales tax; subtract advances paid against either the fee or the expenses; and show a total due. The time for payment would be that specified in Form 2, probably 30 days after delivery of art (although the illustrator could certainly require payment on delivery, if the client is set up to pay that quickly). The title or description of the assignment would be referred to along with the client's purchase order number or the illustrator's job number. Return of the original art would be required. Restating the rights granted would also be wise.

Form 3 really cannot replace Form 1, the Estimate, or Form 2, the Confirmation of Assignment. Waiting until after an assignment is completed to show the terms and conditions which the illustrator wants to govern the assignment is asking for trouble. If the client has not already given the illustrator a form with terms that contradict the invoice, the client may well respond to the terms of the invoice by payment with a check that has writing on its back that contradicts the terms of the invoice. Such a situation is filled with ambiguity and places at risk the business relationship. If the parties review proposed terms prior to working together, a disagreement can be resolved or the parties can agree not to work together on that particular project. Once the work has been done, disagreement over terms is far more difficult to resolve and is likely to leave the kind of bad feeling that makes future ventures dubious.

The invoice repeats almost exactly all the terms which either the estimate or the confirmation of assignment would have contained. As stated above, this would not be necessary if the illustra-tor definitely had a confirmation of assignment signed by both parties. If an estimate alone has been supplied or the client has not signed the estimate or a confirmation of assignment, ambiguity remains as to the terms, and repeating the terms (on the invoice) may be of value, since payment based on the invoice may be viewed by a court or arbitrator as acquiesence to its terms (although this cannot be guaranteed).

The negotiation checklist covers the terms which an invoice would need to contain if a confirmation of assignment has been signed by the client. If a confirmation of assignment has not been signed by the client, the negotiation checklist for Form 2 should also be reviewed.

## Filling in the Form

Use the illustrator's letterhead at the top of the form. Give the date, the client's name and address, the client's purchase order number, and the illustrator's job number. State the fee, expenses to be reimbursed, charges for revisions, advances (in parentheses to show that advances should be subtracted to arrive at the total due); determine the balance, add any necessary sales tax; and show the balance due. In Paragraph 1 describe the assignment briefly. In Paragraph 2, specify when the finished art was delivered. In Paragraph 3 give the limitations on the rights granted and specify whether the client's rights are exclusive or nonexclusive. In Paragraph 5 state the fee. In Paragraph 7 show the amount of any advance paid against expenses. In Paragraph 8 give a monthly interest rate for late payments. Fill in Paragraph 9 if advances on the fee were paid. Check the boxes in Paragraphs 11 and 12 to indicate whether copyright notice or authorship credit will be given in the name of the illustrator. In Paragraph 13 state the percentages of the total fee payable for cancellation at various stages of work. In Paragraph 14 fill in a value for the original art. In Paragraph 16 specify who will arbitrate disputes, where this will be done, and give the maximum amount which can be sued for in small claims court. In Paragraph 17 give the state whose laws will govern the contract. Both parties should then sign the contract.

## Negotiation Checklist

❏ Describe the assignment briefly. (Paragraph 1)

❏ Give the date of delivery of finished art. (Paragraph 2)

❏ State that the grant of rights takes place when the illustrator is paid in full. (Paragraph 3)

❏ Limit the grant of rights and specify whether the client's use of the art will be exclusive or nonexclusive. (Paragraph 3)

❏ Limit the rights granted to finished art only. (Paragraph 3)

❏ All rights not granted to the client should be reserved to the illustrator, including rights in sketches and any other preliminary materials. (Paragraph 4)

❏ The fee plus any sales tax must be specified. (Paragraph 5)

❏ Detail the nature and amount of expenses which the client must reimburse to the illustrator. (Paragraph 7)

❏ State the amount of any advance given against expenses. (Paragraph 7)

❏ Require payment within thirty days of delivery of the finished art. (Paragraph 8)

❏ State the amount of any advances paid against the fee. (Paragraph 9)

❏ If the client has changed the nature of the assignment, additional fees must be charged for revisions. (Paragraph 10)

❏ With respect to revisions or the assignment itself, additional charges might be billed for work which had to be rushed or required unusual hours or other stresses.

❏ State whether the illustrator's copyright notice will appear with the art. (Paragraph 11)

❏ State whether the illustrator will receive name credit with the art. (Paragraph 12)

❏ If authorship credit should be given but is omitted, require payment of an additional fee.

❏ Fees for cancellation at different stages of the assignment should be restated. (Paragraph 13)

❏ State that the illustrator shall own all rights in the work in the event of cancellation. (Paragraph 13)

❏ Specify a time for payment of cancellation fees, such as within thirty days of either the client's stopping work or the delivery of finished art, whichever occurs first. (Paragraph 13)

❏ Specify that if the illustration is not published within a certain time period, the rights shall revert to the illustrator.

❏ State that the illustrator owns the finished art and any preliminary sketches or materials. (Paragraph 14)

❏ If preliminary sketches are published, the fee should increase to the price for finished art.

❏ If physical art is to be sold, a separate price should be specified.

❏ Require the client to return the art within thirty days after use. (Paragraph 14)

❏ Specify a safe method for the return of the art. (Paragraph 14)

❏ Indicate a value for the art, which can serve as a basis for damages if the client does not take reasonable care of it.

❏ Require the client to indemnify the illustrator if the client provides certain materials to be included in the illustration but does not request that the illustrator obtain needed copyright permissions or privacy releases or uses the illustration in a way that exceeds the use allowed by the permissions or releases. (Paragraph 15)

❏ Provide for arbitration, except for amounts which can be sued for in small claims court. (Paragraph 16)

❏ Review the standard provisions in the introductory pages and compare to Paragraph 17.

❏ Especially if the client has not signed Form 2, the Confirmation of Assignment, review the negotiation checklist for Form 2.

< Illustrator's Letterhead >

# Invoice

Client _____  Date _____

Address _____

Client Purchase Order Number _____ Job Number _____

Fee...........................$_____

Expenses................................$_____

Revisions.................................$_____

Advances...............................($_____)

Balance..................................$_____

Sales  tax................................$_____

Balance  due...........................$_____

This Invoice is subject to the the terms and conditions which follow.

**1**. **Description.** The Illustrator has created and delivered to Client _____ illustrations for the following project _____.

**2.** **Delivery Date.** The finished art was delivered on _____, 19_____.

**3.** **Grant of Rights.** Upon receipt of full payment, Illustrator shall grant to the Client the following rights in the finished art:

For use as _____

For the product or publication named _____

In the following territory _____

For the following time period _____

Other limitations _____

With respect to the usage shown above, the Client shall have ❏ exclusive ❏ nonexclusive rights.

If the finished art is for use as a contribution to a magazine, the grant of rights shall be first North American serial rights only unless specified to the contrary above.

**4.** **Reservation of Rights.** All rights not expressly granted are reserved to the Illustrator, including but not limited to all rights in sketches, comps, or other preliminary materials.

**5.** **Fee.** Client shall pay the following purchase price: $_____ for the usage rights granted. Client shall also pay sales tax, if required.

**6.** **Additional Usage.** If Client wishes to make any additional uses of the Work, Client shall seek permission from the Illustrator and pay an additional fee to be agreed upon.

**7. Expenses.** If Illustrator incurred reimbursable expenses, a listing of such expenses is attached to this Invoice with copies of supporting documentation. Illustrator has received $_____ as an advance against expenses.

**8. Payment.** Payment is due to the Illustrator within thirty days of the date of this Invoice, which is dated as of the date of delivery of the finished art. Overdue payments shall be subject to interest charges of _____ percent monthly.

**9. Advances.** Illustrator received $_____ as an advance against the total fee.

**10. Revisions.** The Illustrator shall be given the first opportunity to make any revisions requested by the Client. If the revisions are not due to any fault on the part of the Illustrator, an additional fee shall be charged. If the Illustrator objects to any revisions to be made by the Client, the Illustrator shall have the right to have his or her name removed from the published Work.

**11. Copyright Notice.** Copyright notice in the name of the Illustrator ❏ shall ❏ shall not accompany the Work when it is reproduced.

**12. Authorship Credit.** Authorship credit in the name of the Illustrator ❏ shall ❏ shall not accompany the Work when it is reproduced. If the finished art is used as a contribution to a magazine or for a book, authorship credit shall be given unless specified to the contrary in the preceding sentence.

**13. Cancellation.** In the event of cancellation by the Client, the amount charged to the Client as the fee in this Invoice has been computed as follows based on the fee originally agreed upon: **(A)** Cancellation prior to the finished art being turned in: ____ percent of fee; **(B)** Cancellation due to finished art being unsatisfactory: ____ percent of fee; and **(C)** Cancellation for any other reason after the finished art is turned in: ____ percent of fee. In the event of cancellation, the Client shall pay any expenses incurred by the Illustrator and the Illustrator shall own all rights in the Work. The Invoice upon cancellation is payable within thirty days of the Client's notification to stop work or the delivery of the finished art, whichever occurs sooner.

**14. Ownership and Return of Artwork.** The ownership of original artwork, including sketches and any other materials created in the process of making the finished art, shall remain with the Illustrator. All such artwork shall be returned to the Illustrator by bonded messenger, air freight, or registered mail within thirty days of the Client's completing its use of the artwork. A reasonable value for the original, finished art is $_____.

**15. Permissions and Releases.** The Client shall indemnify and hold harmless the Illustrator against any and all claims, costs, and expenses, including attorney's fees, due to materials included in the Work at the request of the Client for which no copyright permission or privacy release was requested or uses which exceed the uses allowed pursuant to a permission or release.

**16. Arbitration.** All disputes shall be submitted to binding arbitration before _____ in the following location _____ and settled in accordance with the rules of the American Arbitration Association. Judgment upon the arbitration award may be entered in any court having jurisdiction thereof. Disputes in which the amount at issue is less than $_____ shall not be subject to this arbitration provision.

**17. Miscellany.** This Invoice shall be governed by the laws of the State of _____.

Illustrator _____

# Illustrator—Agent Contract

**A**n agent can be of immeasurable value to an illustrator. Instead of seeking assignments, the illustrator can devote full time to creative work and trust that the agent will provide marketing impetus. The cost to the illustrator is the agent's commission, which is usually 25 percent, but the hope is that the agent will enable the illustrator to earn more. The agent may have better contacts and be able to secure a better quality of client and more remunerative assignments.

The agent should not be given markets in which the agent cannot effectively sell. For example, an agent in New York may not be able to sell in Los Angeles or London. Nor should the agent be given exclusivity in markets in which the illustrator may want to sell or want to have other agents sell. The length of the contract should not be overly long, or should be subject to a right of termination on notice. While the agent may promise to use best efforts, such a promise is almost impossible to enforce. If the agent fails to sell, the illustrator must take over sales or find another agent.

Promotion is an important aspect of the agent's work for the illustrator. The illustrator will have to provide sufficient samples for the agent to work effectively. Beyond this, direct mail campaigns and paid advertising in promotional directories may gain clients. The sharing of such promotional expenses must be agreed to between the illustrator and agent.

One sticky issue can be house accounts; clients of the illustrator not obtained by the agent. Both the definition of house accounts and the commission paid to the agent on such accounts must be negotiated. Termination raises another difficult issue, since the agent may feel that commissions should continue to be paid for assignments obtained after termination from clients originally contacted by the agent. There are several approaches to resolve this. The agent may be given a continuing right to commissions for a limited time depending on how long the representation lasted. Or the illustrator may make a payout to the agent, either in a lump sum or in installments over several years. If the relationship was brief and unsuccessful, of course, the agent should have no rights at termination except to collect commissions for assignments obtained prior to termination.

The agent would usually handle billings and provide accountings. The illustrator would want to be able to review the books and records of the agent. Since both the illustrator and agent provide personal services, the contract should not be assignable.

A distinction has to be made between an agent obtaining assignments and obtaining a book contract. The agent for an author receives a commission of 10 to 15 percent, compared to the 25 percent charged by an illustrator's agent. If an agent arranges an assignment for a book jacket or a limited number of illustrations in a book, the 25 percent commission is reasonable. But if the illustrator is to be the author or coauthor of a book, it might be fairer to reduce the commission to the 10 to 15 percent range. One consideration might be whether the illustrator receives a flat fee or a royalty, since a royalty makes the illustrator more like an author.

A good source to locate agents is the membership list for the Society of Photographer and Artist Representatives (SPAR), P.O. Box 845, FDR Station, New York, New York 10017.

## Filling in the Form

In the Preamble fill in the date and the names and addresses of the illustrator and agent. In Paragraph 1 indicate the geographical area and markets in which the agent will represent the illustrator and whether the representation will be exclusive or nonexclusive. In Paragraph 5 fill in the commission rates. In Paragraph 6 check the party responsible for billings. In Paragraph 7 indicate the time for payment after receipt of fees and the interest rate for late payments. In Paragraph 8 indicate how promotional expenses will be shared. In Paragraph 11 state when and for how long the agent shall have a right to commissions after termination. In Paragraph 13 give the names of arbitrators and the place for arbitration, as well as the maximum amount which can be sued for in small claims court. In Paragraph 17 fill in which state's laws will govern the contract. Both parties should sign the contract and, if necessary, fill in the Schedule of House Accounts by listing the names and addresses of clients.

## Negotiation Checklist

❏ Limit the scope of the agent's represention by geography and types of markets. (Paragraph 1)

❏ State whether the representation is exclusive or nonexclusive. (Paragraph 1) If the representation is exclusive, the agent will have a right to commissions on assignments obtained by other agents. Assignments obtained by the illustrator would fall under the house-account provision in Paragraph 5.

❏ If the agent uses other agents for certain markets (for example, for foreign sales or film sales), review the impact of this on commissions.

❏ Limit the types of art the contract covers.

❏ State that sales through galleries or sales of original art in general are not within the scope of the agency agreement.

❏ Any rights not granted to the agent should be reserved to the illustrator. (Paragraph 1)

❏ Require that the agent use best efforts to sell the work of the illustrator. (Paragraph 2)

❏ State that the agent shall keep the illustrator promptly and regularly informed with respect to negotiations and other matters, and shall submit all offers to the illustrator.

❏ State that any contract negotiated by the agent is not binding unless signed by the illustrator.

❏ If the illustrator is willing to give the agent power of attorney so the agent can sign on behalf of the illustrator, the power of attorney should be very specific as to what rights the agent can exercise.

❏ Require that the agent keep confidential all matters handled for the illustrator.

❏ Give the illustrator the right to accept or reject any assignment obtained by the agent. (Paragraph 2)

❏ Specify the samples to be supplied to the agent by the illustrator. (Paragraph 3)

❏ If the samples are valuable, agree as to their value.

❏ Require the agent to insure the samples at the value agreed to.

❏ Raise the agent's responsibility for the samples to strict liability for any loss or damage.

❏ Provide for a short term, such as one year. (Paragraph 4) This interplays with the termination provision. Since termination is permitted on thirty days notice in Paragraph 11, the length of the term is of less importance in this contract.

❏ If the contract has a relatively long term and cannot be terminated on notice at any time, allow termination if the agent fails to generate a certain level of sales on a quarterly, semiannual, or annual basis.

❏ If the contract has a relatively long term and cannot be terminated on notice at any time, allow for termination if the specific agent dies or leaves the agency.

❏ Specify the commission percentage for assignments obtained by the agent during the term of the contract. This is usually 25 percent of the fee, and may be 2 1/2 to 5 percent higher for out-of-town assignments.

❏ Define house accounts, probably as accounts obtained by other agents prior to the contract or obtained by the illustrator at any time, and specify the commission to be paid on such accounts. A reasonable commission might be 10 percent, especially if the agent does the billing. The illustrator may not want to pay any commission on these accounts, while the agent may want the full commission. (Paragraph 5)

❏ List house accounts by name on the Statement of House Accounts. This can be supplemented if house accounts are developed after the contract is signed. (Paragraph 5)

❏ State that the commission shall be computed on the billing less any expenses incurred by the illustrator, especially if expenses are substantial and are not reimbursed by the client. (Paragraph 5)

❏ State that commissions are not payable on billings which have not been collected. (Paragraph 5)

❏ Confirm that the agent will not collect a commission for the illustrator's speaking fees, grants, or prizes.

❏ Distinguish between an assignment to contribute to a book and being the author or coauthor of a book. Agents representing authors charge 10 to 15 percent of proceeds from the book as the commission. While the dividing line may be a fine one, illustrators likely to make substantial contributions to a book should consider whether treatment as an author may be appropriate in terms of the agent's commission rate. (Paragraph 5)

❏ In the case of an agent for a book, consider letting the agency do only that particular title or project.

❏ Determine who will bill and collect from the client. This would usually be a service provided by the agent. (Paragraph 6)

❏ Give the illustrator the right to collect his or her share directly from clients. This might provide some protection against the agent's insolvency or holding of money in the event of a dispute. Usually, the illustrator would want the agent to collect billings.

❏ Require payments to be made quickly after billings are collected. (Paragraph 7)

❏ Charge interest on payments that are overdue. (Paragraph 7)

❏ Require the agent to treat money due the illustrator as trust funds and to hold it in an account separate from the funds of the agency. (Paragraph 7)

❏ Share promotional expenses, such as direct mail campaigns or paid page advertising in directories. The agent may contribute 25 percent or more to these expenses. (Paragraph 8)

❏ State that both parties must agree before promotional expenses may be incurred by the agent. (Paragraph 8)

❏ Require the agent to pay for a specified minimum amount of promotional expenses, perhaps without any sharing on the part of the illustrator.

❏ If expenses incurred by the agent benefit several illustrators, be certain there is a fair allocation of expenses to each illustrator.

❏ Require the agent to bear miscellaneous marketing expenses, such as messengers, shipping, and the like. (Paragraph 8)

❏ If the agent insists that the illustrator bear certain expenses, require the illustrator's approval for expenses in excess of a minimum amount.

❏ State that the illustrator shall receive a copy of the invoice given to the client at the time the illustrator is paid. (Paragraph 9)

❏ Provide for full accountings on a regular basis, such as every six months, if requested. (Paragraph 9)

❏ Provide the right to inspect books and records on reasonable notice. (Paragraph 10)

❏ Allow for termination on thirty days notice to the other party. (Paragraph 11)

❏ State that the agreement will terminate in the event of the agent's bankruptcy or insolvency. (Paragraph 11)

❏ If termination occurs, specify for how long, if at all, the agent will receive commissions from assignments obtained by the illustrator from clients developed by the agent during the time the contract was in effect. (Paragraph 11) For example, if the agency contract lasted for less than a year, the agent might have such a right for three months after termination. If the agency contract lasted more than a year but less than two years, the right might continue for six months after termination. If the agent has a right to commissions after termination for too long a period, the illustrator may find it difficult to find another agent.

❏ Instead of allowing the agent to collect commissions for some period of time after termination, a fixed amount might be stated in the original contract. For example, 20 percent of the average annual billings for the prior 3 years might be payable in 3 installments over a year. The percentages and payment schedule are negotiable, but the illustrator must avoid any agreement which would make it difficult either to earn a living or find another agent. The percentage to be paid might increase if the agent has represented the illustrator for a longer period (or decrease for a shorter period), but should be subject to a cap or maximum amount.

❏ Do not give the agent any rights to commissions from house accounts after termination.

❏ For book contracts, it is customary for the agent to continue to collect royalties and deduct the agent's commission even after termination of the agency contract. However, it would be better for the illustrator to have the right to direct payment of his or her share after such termination.

❏ Do not allow assignment of the contract, since both the agent and the illustrator are rendering personal services. (Paragraph 12)

❏ Allow the illustrator to assign payments due under the contract. (Paragraph 12)

❏ If the agent represents illustrators who are competitive with one another, decide what precautions might be taken against favoritism. Whether it is advantageous or disadvantageous to have an agent represent competing talent will depend on the unique circumstances of each case.

❏ If the agent requires a warranty and indemnity clause under which the illustrator states that he or she owns the work and has the right to sell it, limit the liability of the illustrator to actual breaches resulting in a judgment and try to place a ceiling on the potential liability.

❏ Provide for arbitration of disputes in excess of the amount which can be sued for in small claims court. (Paragraph 13)

❏ If there is an arbitration provision, consider specifying the Joint Ethics Committee in New York City or a similar group near the illustrator's location to act as arbitrator.

❏ Compare the standard provisions in the introductory pages with Paragraphs 14-17.

The schedule of house accounts, which lists the names and addresses of clients, is not shown here. It is included with the tear-out form.

# Illustrator—Agent Contract

AGREEMENT, entered into as of this _____ day of _____, 19_____, between _____ (hereinafter referred to as the "Illustrator"), located at _____, and _____ (hereinafter referred to as the "Agent"), located at _____.

WHEREAS, the Illustrator is an established illustrator of proven talents; and

WHEREAS, the Illustrator wishes to have an agent represent him or her in marketing certain rights enumerated herein; and

WHEREAS, the Agent is capable of marketing the artwork produced by the Illustrator; and

WHEREAS, the Agent wishes to represent the Illustrator;

NOW, THEREFORE, in consideration of the foregoing premises and the mutual covenants hereinafter set forth and other valuable consideration, the parties hereto agree as follows:

1. **Agency**. The Illustrator appoints the Agent to act as his or her representative:

   **(A)** in the following geographical area _____

   **(B)** for the following markets:

   - ❑ Advertising
   - ❑ Corporate
   - ❑ Book publishing
   - ❑ Magazines
   - ❑ Other, specified as _____

   **(C)** to be the Illustrator's ❑ exclusive ❑ nonexclusive agent in the area and markets indicated.

   Any rights not granted to the Agent are reserved to the Illustrator.

2. **Best Efforts.** The Agent agrees to use his or her best efforts in submitting the Illustrator's work for the purpose of securing assignments for the Illustrator. The Agent shall negotiate the terms of any assignment that is offered, but the Illustrator may reject any assignment if he or she finds the terms thereof unacceptable.

3. **Samples.** The Illustrator shall provide the Agent with such samples of work as are from time to time necessary for the purpose of securing assignments. These samples shall remain the property of the Illustrator and be returned on termination of this Agreement. The Agent shall take reasonable efforts to protect the work from loss or damage, but shall be liable for such loss or damage only if caused by the Agent's negligence.

4. **Term.** This Agreement shall take effect as of the date first set forth above, and remain in full force and effect for a term of one year, unless terminated as provided in Paragraph 11.

5. **Commissions.** The Agent shall be entitled to the following commissions: **(A)** On assignments obtained by the Agent during the term of this Agreement, _____ percent of the billing. **(B)** On house accounts, _____ percent of the billing. For purposes of this Agreement, house accounts are defined as accounts obtained by the Illustrator at any time or obtained by another agent representing the Illustrator prior to the commencement of this Agreement and are listed in the Schedule of House Accounts attached to this Agreement. **(C)** For books which the Illustrator authors or coauthors, _____ percent of the royalties or licensing proceeds paid to the Illustrator by the publisher or its licensees.

   It is understood by both parties that no commissions shall be paid on assignments rejected by the Illustrator or for which the Illustrator fails to receive payment, regardless of the reason payment is not made. Further, no commissions shall be payable in either **(A)** or **(B)** above for any part of the billing that is due to expenses incurred by the Illustrator in performing the assignment, whether or not such expenses are reimbursed by the client. In the event that a flat fee is paid by the client, it shall be reduced by the amount of expenses incurred by the Illustrator in performing the assignment, and the Agent's commission shall be payable only on the fee as reduced for expenses.

**6. Billing.** The ❏ Illustrator ❏ Agent shall be responsible for all billings.

**7. Payments.** The party responsible for billing shall make all payments due within _____ days of receipt of any fees covered by this Agreement. Such payments due shall be be deemed trust funds and shall not be inter-mingled with funds belonging to the party responsible for billing and payment. Late payments shall be accom-panied by interest calculated at the rate of _____ percent per month thereafter.

**8. Promotional Expenses.** Promotional expenses, including but not limited to promotional mailings and paid advertising, shall be mutually agreed to by the parties and paid _____ percent by the Agent and _____ per-cent by the Illustrator. The Agent shall bear the expenses of shipping, insurance, and similar marketing expenses.

**9. Accountings.** The party responsible for billing shall send copies of invoices to the other party when rendered. If requested, that party shall also provide the other party with semiannual accountings showing all assignments for the period, the clients' names and addresses, the fees paid, expenses incurred by the Illustrator, the dates of payment, the amounts on which the Agent's commissions are to be calculated, and the sums due less those amounts already paid.

**10. Inspection of the Books and Records.** The party responsible for the billing shall keep the books and records with respect to payments due each party at his or her place of business and permit the other party to inspect these books and records during normal business hours on the giving of reasonable notice.

**11. Termination.** This Agreement may be terminated by either party by giving thirty (30) days written notice to the other party. If the Illustrator receives assignments after the termination date from clients originally obtained by the Agent during the term of this Agreement, the commission specified in Paragraph 5(A) shall be payable to the Agent under the following circumstances. If the Agent has represented the Illustrator for _____ months or less, the Agent shall receive a commission on such assignments received by the Illustrator within _____ days of the date of termination. This period shall increase by thirty (30) days for each additional _____ months that the Agent has represented the Illustrator, but in no event shall such period exceed _____ days. In the event of the bankruptcy or insolvency of the Agent, this Agreement shall also terminate. The rights and obligations under Paragraphs 3, 6, 7, 8, 9, and 10 shall survive termination.

**12. Assignment.** This Agreement shall not be assigned by either of the parties hereto. It shall be binding on and inure to the benefit of the successors, admininstrators, executors, or heirs of the Agent and Illustrator.

**13. Arbitration.** Any disputes arising under this Agreement shall be settled by arbitration before _____ under the rules of the American Arbitration Association in the City of _____, except that the par-ties shall have the right to go to court for claims of $_____ or less. Any award rendered by the arbitrator may be entered in any court having jurisdiction thereof.

**14. Notices.** All notices shall be given to the parties at their respective addresses set forth above.

**15. Independent Contractor Status.** Both parties agree that the Agent is acting as an independent contractor. This Agreement is not an employment agreement, nor does it constitute a joint venture or partnership between the Illustrator and Agent.

**16. Amendments and Merger.** All amendments to this Agreement must be written. This Agreement incorporates the entire understanding of the parties.

**17. Governing Law.** This Agreement shall be governed by the laws of the State of _____ .

IN WITNESS WHEREOF, the parties have signed this Agreement as of the date set forth above.

Illustrator_____      Agent_____

# Book Publishing Contract

**A** book contract is worth celebrating, but it is like a celebration to mark the beginning of a long journey. The creation of the book may take years, the life of the book may span decades. And the book may be the source for innumerable spinoffs, such as a television series, films, and even the licensing of characters for merchandise.

The book contract offers opportunities and presents pitfalls. Illustrators are well advised to seek expert assistance in negotiating these contracts. Since the book contract invariably originates with the publisher, the negotiation checklist will be especially valuable. Form 5 is worth study because it contains terms which are favorable to illustrators.

Form 5 might also be used when a nonprofessional publisher asks an illustrator to do a book. For example, a charity, chamber of commerce, or even a corporation might want to contract for a book of specialized interest. If neither party has a standard contract to offer, Form 5 could be adapted for use.

The grant of rights gives the publisher certain rights, which the illustrator carefully seeks to limit with respect to medium, time period, territory, and language. Beyond this, however, the publisher also seeks subsidiary rights, which are simply rights of exploitation in markets not encompassed by the grant of rights. If the grant of rights covers only the publication of books, then the sale of film or audio versions would be a licensing of subsidiary rights.

The goal of the illustrator in negotiating a book contract is to give the publisher only those rights that the publisher is capable of successfully exploiting. For those rights given to the publisher, fair compensation must be provided by the contract. Compensation usually takes the form of an advance and a royalty, so that the illustrator profits from greater sales of the work. Advances are paid to the illustrator in installments, often half when the contract is signed and half when the manuscript is turned in to the publisher.

Accountings should take place on a regular basis and provide the illustrator with as much information as possible.

Because compensation to the illustrator is based on royalties, the computation of the royalty is crucial. First, is the royalty based on retail price or net price? Most publishers compute royalties based on retail price, which is best for authors. Net price is what the publisher receives from selling the book to wholesalers and bookstores, so net price is usually 40 to 50 percent less than retail price. The percentage rates for royalties are crucial. While these rates are subject to negotiation, somewhat standard rates are given in the negotiation checklist. And there is one important piece of information that many authors are not aware of. That is, royalty rates are reduced for a number of reasons, such as sales at a higher-than-normal discount. These reductions can have a devastating effect on royalties. The contract must be carefully reviewed to ascertain the impact of such royalty reduction provisions.

The illustrator will want to have the work copyrighted in the illustrator's name. The copyright lasts for the life of the illustrator plus another fifty years and any publishing contract can be terminated after thirty-five to forty years under the termination provisions of the copyright law. To avoid any confusion as to who owns the copyright, the copyright notice in the book should be in the illustrator's name.

The illustrator will also want artistic control over the content of the book. No changes should be allowed without the illustrator's approval. Certainly no advertising or unrelated content should be added without the consent of the illustrator. The publisher will request a warranty and indemnity provision from the illustrator. In this provision the illustrator states that the book contains no copyright infringements, no defamatory material, invades no one's privacy, and is not otherwise unlawful. If any of these warranties prove incorrect, the illustrator agrees to reimburse the publisher for any damages and costs, including attorney's fees. Some publishers are now extending their publishers' liability insurance to cover illustrators for these risks. In the absence of such insurance, the illustrator should seek to set a dollar limit or percent-of-royalty-income ceiling on his or her liability to the publisher. The publisher will also want the option to publish the illustrator's next work and will want to restrict the illustrator from publishing competing works. The illustrator should certainly try to have both these provisions stricken from the contract, since they may impair the illustrator's ability to earn a livelihood.

If an illustrator is creating a book with an author, many publishers will simply have both the illustrator and author sign a book contract which specifies the division of royalties. This is satisfactory for the publisher, but leaves unresolved many important issues between the illustrator and author. They should have a collaboration agreement, such as that shown in Form 6.

## Filling in the Form

In the Preamble, fill in the date and the names and addresses of the parties. In the first Whereas clause, briefly describe the subject of the book. In Paragraph 1 enter the title of the book and specify the rights granted to the publisher with respect to form (such as hardcover, quality paperback, mass market paperback), territory, language, and term. In Paragraph 3 fill in the deadline for delivery of the manuscript as well as the approximate length of the book. Provide the amount of time to do revisions if requested and, in the event of rejection of the manuscript, specify what will happen to advances which have been paid. In Paragraph 4 fill in whatever materials, such as illustrations or an index, the illustrator is also obligated to provide and specify a contribution by the publisher toward these costs. In Paragraph 5 specify a contribution by the publisher toward the costs of obtaining any permissions. In Paragraph 6 give the number of months in which the publisher must publish the book. In Paragraph 7 specify the royalty rates and situations in which royalties are discounted. In Paragraph 8 fill in the subsidiary rights which the publisher has the right to license and the division of income for each right. In Paragraph 9 specify the amount of the advance to the illustrator. Indicate in Paragraph 10 how often the publisher will give accountings. In Paragraph 13 show the form of authorship credit which the illustrator will receive. In Paragraph 14 place limits on how much the illustrator can be forced to pay for a breach of warranty and how much the publisher can hold in escrow to cover the illustrator's indemnity obligation. State in Paragraph 15 which artistic decisions will be determined by the illustrator. In Paragraph 17 specify how many free copies the illustrator will receive and give the discount at which the illustrator may purchase additional copies. In Paragraph 24 state who will arbitrate and the place for arbitration. In Paragraph 28 fill in which state's law will govern the contract. Both parties should then sign the contract.

## Negotiation Checklist

❑ Limit the grant of exclusive rights to publish with respect to medium, area, duration, and language, such as granting "book rights in the English language in the United States for a term of ten years." Note that publishers will want to expand the grant of rights and exploit the book over the long life of the copyright. (Paragraph 1)

❑ Consider reserving Canadian rights, in particular, for sale to a Canadian publisher.

❑ Specify with respect to medium whether the grant of rights covers hardcover, quality paperback, mass market paperback, etc.

❑ Reserve to the illustrator all rights not specifically granted to the publisher. (Paragraph 2)

❏ Specify a date for delivery of the manuscript. (Paragraph 3)

❏ Do not make time of the essence with respect to delivery of the manuscript.

❏ Extend the deadline in the event of the illness of the illustrator or other circumstances beyond his or her control which cause a delay.

❏ Provide for a margin of lateness in delivery, such as ninety days, before the publisher can terminate the agreement. (Paragraph 3) Any extensions of the time for delivery should be obtained in writing.

❏ Give the approximate length in words of the manuscript to be delivered. (Paragraph 3)

❏ Allow the illustrator to deliver a "complete manuscript," rather than "a manuscript in form and content satisfactory to the publisher." (Paragraph 3 offers a compromise.)

❏ If the illustrator must deliver a manuscript which is satisfactory to the publisher, make an objective standard of reasonableness such as "reasonably satisfactory."

❏ Attach an outline or detailed description of the book to the contract so the manuscript can be judged against the outline. (Paragraph 3)

❏ Require the publisher to give detailed suggestions for revisions and a reasonable time to do the revisions. (Paragraph 3)

❏ If the manuscript is rejected by the publisher, determine whether advances will be kept, paid back, or paid back only if another contract for the book is signed with a different publisher. (Paragraph 3)

❏ If the illustrator is submitting portions of the work in progress, have the publisher confirm in writing that these portions are satisfactory.

❏ Specify whether the illustrator shall be responsible for delivering illustrations, photographs, maps, tables, charts, or an index, and give details as to the number and nature of any such additional items. (Paragraph 4)

❏ If the illustrator must provide additional items which require the outlay of money, such as photographs or having an index created, state who will pay for this. (Paragraph 4)

❏ If the illustrator is to pay for such additional items, such as an index or permission fees, have the publisher make a nonrefundable payment toward these costs. (Paragraph 4)

❏ If the illustrator is to create the index, allow for a certain amount of time in which to do this after the illustrator has the paginated galleys.

❏ If the illustrator fails to deliver any required materials, allow for a certain period of time, such as thirty days after notice from the publisher, in which the illustrator can provide what is missing.

❏ Require the publisher to publish the book within a certain time period, such as twelve or eighteen months. (Paragraph 6)

❏ If the publisher does not publish within the specified time period, give the illustrator the right to terminate the contract and keep all money received. (Paragraph 6)

❏ Provide for royalties, which are usually preferable to a flat fee. (Paragraph 7)

❏ If a flat fee is offered, require a reuse fee after a certain number of books are printed so the flat fee becomes more like a royalty.

❏ Base the computation of royalties on suggested retail price, not net price which is what the publisher receives from wholesalers and book stores. (Paragraph 7)

❏ If the contract provides for a freight pass-through (in which a book is priced at a slightly higher price to reimburse the bookstore for freight costs which the publisher normally pays but is not, in fact, paying), indicate that the amount of the freight pass-through is to be subtracted from the retail price prior to the computation of royalties.

❏ Have the royalty be a percentage of retail price, rather than a fixed dollar amount, since the price of the book may increase over time. (Paragraph 7)

All royalties are negotiable and the rates offered vary from one publisher to another, but what follows are general guidelines of what the illustrator may expect:

❏ For an adult trade book in hardcover, a basic royalty of 10 percent of suggested retail price on the first 5,000 copies sold, 12 1/2 percent on the next 5,000 copies, and 15 percent on all copies sold in excess of 10,000.

❏ For a children's book in hardcover, a basic royalty starting at 10 percent and escalating to 15 percent after an agreed upon number of copies are sold (but the practice varies widely with respect to children's books).

❏ For a quality paperback published by the publisher of the hardcover edition or as a paperback original, a royalty of 6 percent of retail price on the first 10,000 copies (or the first print run if it is less than 10,000 copies) with an increase to 7 1/2 percent for copies sold in excess of 10,000. Some publishers may offer 8 to 10 percent as a royalty, while others may escalate their rates only after the sale of 25,000 copies.

❏ For a mass market paperback published by the publisher of the hardcover edition, a royalty of 6 percent of retail price on the first 150,000 copies sold with an increase to 8 percent thereafter. A mass market original may have a similar or somewhat higher royalty rate structure.

❏ For professional, scientific, or technical books, a royalty is likely to be based on net price (which is what the publisher receives) rather than retail price. The royalty should be at least 15 percent of the net price. For hardcover textbooks, the royalty should escalate to 18 percent after 7,500 or 10,000 books have been sold and go even higher thereafter.

❏ For textbooks which originate in paperback, the royalty should be in the range of 10 to 15 percent of net price.

❏ Whenever escalations in royalty rates are provided in a contract, review carefully which sales are counted to reach the number of copies necessary for the royalty to escalate.

❏ Review with special care any provisions which reduce royalties and find out how many sales are likely to come within these provisions.

❏ Establish that the reduced royalties will in no event be less than half or three-quarters of what the regular royalties would have been.

Sales causing reduced royalties may include:

❏ Sales at a higher than normal discount to wholesalers or retailers. A normal discount might be 40 percent, and some publishers reduce royalties when the discount reaches 48 percent or more. This reduction may be gradual, such as 1 percent of royalty for each percent in excess of 48 percent discount, but the impact can be great. Moving the starting point for reductions from a 48 percent discount to perhaps a 51 percent discount may minimize the loss to a large degree, depending on the sales structure of the particular publisher. If such discounts are due to purchasing large quantities of books, the illustrator should also consider requiring that different titles not be cumulated together for these purposes. Such cumulation has little to do with the sale of the illustrator's books.

❏ Sales by mail order or direct response advertising may cause the royalty to be reduced to as little as half the regular royalty rate.

❏ Sales in Canada may cause the royalty to be reduced to two-thirds or even half of the regular royalty rate.

❏ Sales on small reprintings, such as 1,000 copies, may cause the royalty to be reduced to three-quarters of the regular rate. The illustrator might allow this only if sales in the period prior to the reprinting were below a certain level and the reprinting did not take place until two years after first publication.

❏ Childrens' book illustrators should pay especially close attention to royalty reductions for sales in library bound editions outside normal trade channels.

❏ Sales for export, to reading circles, to book clubs, and to organizations outside regular book-selling channels, may, if the discount from retail price is 60 percent or greater, cause the royalty to be reduced to 15 percent (for bound copies) or 18 percent (for unbound sheets) of what the publisher actually receives.

❏ Sales as a remainder (when excess inventory is liquidated), if at a discount of 70 percent of more, may cause the royalty to be reduced to 10 percent of what the publisher actually receives (or no royalty at all if the price is less than the publisher's manufacturing cost).

❏ Limit the percentage of copies which can be treated as sold at a discount.

❏ For royalties based on what the publisher actually receives, do not allow any reduction for discounts or bad debts.

❏ Finally, with respect to reduced royalties, promotional copies, author's copies, and copies which are destroyed are royalty free.

❏ Consider requiring that the publisher of the hardcover not bring out a paperback version until one year after the hardcover publication.

❏ Determine as to each subsidiary right which party controls that right and what the division of proceeds will be. (Paragraph 8) Subsidiary rights cover many possible sources of income which the publisher will exploit through marketing to other companies. Licensing of subsidiary rights may include abridgments, book clubs, reprints by another publisher, first and second serializations (which are magazine or newspaper rights before and after book publication), foreign or translation rights, syndication, advertising, commercial uses, films, plays, radio shows, television, audio tapes, and other mechanical renditions.

❏ State that the publisher has no right to share in subsidiary rights if the publisher does not fulfill all of its obligations under the contract. (Paragraph 8)

❏ Determine for each right whether the illustrator, agent, or publisher can best sell that right.

❏ Reserve to the illustrator all rights the publisher is not set up to sell.

❏ Retain a right of approval over subsidiary rights to be sold by the publisher.

❏ Reserve to the illustrator all nonpublishing rights, such as stage, audio tapes, television, and film. This should include commercial rights, such as the right to make art into posters, stationery, calendars, toys, apparel, and other merchandise.

❏ For first serial sales (the sale of part of the book to a magazine before first publication of the book), the illustrator should receive 100 percent of the income. If the publisher acts as agent, the publisher might receive 10 to 20 percent. This approach would also apply to nonpublishing rights if, in fact, the publisher does obtain a right to share in the proceeds.

❏ For paperback licenses, book club licenses, abridgments and selections, and second serializations (the sale of part of the book to a magazine after first publication of the book), the illustrator should seek 50 percent of the first $10,000 of income, 60 percent of the next $10,000, and 70 percent over $20,000.

❏ For microfilm or computer uses, the illustrator should seek 50 percent of the income.

❏ If the original publication is in paperback, the illustrator should expect 50 to 75 percent of the income from licensing hardcover rights.

❏ For a paperback original, consider requiring that the paperback publisher wait a year before licensing hardcover rights.

❏ Allow the illustrator 120 days to seek out a better offer for a paperback reprint.

❏ Carefully scrutinize the definition of licensing income. The illustrator should always seek to have no reductions from such income. If the publisher uses "net income," the illustrator must check which expenses will be deducted.

❏ Require that the illustrator receive copies of any licenses negotiated by the publisher.

❏ Provide for the pass-through of licensing income received (perhaps in excess of a specified minimum amount, such as $100), so that such income is paid to the illustrator within 10 days of receipt by the publisher and is not held for payment with other royalties.

❏ Provide for the payment of nonrefundable

advances to the illustrator, preferably paid in full at the time of signing the contract or half on signing the contract and half on delivery of the manuscript. (Paragraph 9)

❏ Provide that each book project is separate, so that money owed by the illustrator on one book cannot be taken from money due to the illustrator on another book.

❏ Consider whether income from licensing subsidiary rights, especially first serial rights, should be applied to unearned advances.

❏ Require periodic accountings at least every six months, which is common for the publishing industry, or as frequently as every three months if it can be negotiated. (Paragraph 10)

❏ Specify the information to be given in the accountings, so the illustrator can appraise their accuracy. Ideally the accounting would show for the period and cumulatively to date the number of copies printed and bound, copies sold and returned at each royalty rate, copies distributed free for publicity, copies lost or destroyed, copies remaindered, and royalties due to the illustrator. (Paragraph 10)

❏ Income from subsidiary rights should also be accounted for on these statements, even if such income is passed through to the illustrator on receipt by the publisher. Copies of licenses should be provided at this time, if they have not already been provided.

❏ If the publisher wishes to create a reserve against returns of books, the amount of this reserve should be limited to a percentage of royalties due in any period (such as 20 percent) and the reserve should not be allowed to continue beyond a specified number of accounting periods. Since sales on first publication are most likely to be returned, the reserve might last for 3 accounting periods after first publication. (Paragraph 10)

❏ Require that any sums owing on the statements of account be paid when the statements are given. (Paragraph 11)

❏ In a very unusual case, after careful consultation with a tax adviser, the illustrator may want a provision which limits royalties each year and causes any additional royalties to be spread forward into the future. In general, this is unwise.

❏ State that the illustrator has a right to inspect the books and records of the publisher and, if a discrepancy of more than 5 percent is found to the publisher's advantage, the publisher shall pay the cost of the inspection. (Paragraph 12)

❏ Do not allow the publisher to place a time limit, such as one or two years after the mailing of the statement of account, on the illustrator's right to inspect the books and have errors corrected.

❏ Require that copyright notice appear in the name of the illustrator. (Paragraph 13)

❏ Require the publisher to register the copyright. (Paragraph 13)

❏ Specify that the illustrator shall receive authorship credit. If there is a coauthor, indicate the sequence of names and, if necessary, size and placement. (Paragraph 13)

❏ Seek to have the publisher cover the illustrator under the publisher's liability insurance policy for copyright infringements, libel, and related violations of rights. This will safeguard the illustrator against many of the dangers in the warranty and indemnity provisions of publishers' contracts.

❏ If the publisher covers the illustrator with its insurance, seek to have the publisher also pay or at least share in the cost of any deductible (which may be as high as $50,000 or $100,000) in the event of a claim.

❏ State that the illustrator only warrants that to his or her knowledge the work does not libel anyone or violate their rights of privacy. (Paragraph 14)

❏ Limit the indemnification to final judgments after all appeals have been taken. Avoid indemnifying for alleged breaches of the warranties. (Paragraph 14)

❏ Reserve the right not to pay for the publisher's costs and attorney's fees if the illustrator selects and pays for the attorney to defend the action. (Paragraph 14)

❏ Do not indemnify for materials inserted at the publisher's request. (Paragraph 14)

❏ Require that the publisher indemnify the illustrator for materials inserted in the book or placed on the cover at the publisher's request or choice.

❏ Limit the amount of the illustrator's indemnification to the lesser of a dollar amount or a percentage of amounts payable under the contract. (Paragraph 14)

❏ Limit the right of the publisher to withhold royalties on account of the lawsuit to the lesser of a percentage of amounts payable under the contract or the amount of alleged damages. (Paragraph 14) Alternatively, the illustrator might seek the right to post a surety bond.

❏ Do not agree to let sums payable under one contract be used to pay for a breach of a warranty under another contract.

❏ Retain a veto power over any settlements to be entered into by the publisher, since the money to pay the settlement may be the illustrator's.

❏ If there is a joint author, determine whether both illustrator and author will be liable for a breach of warranty by one or the other. Review Form 6.

❏ Keep artistic control over the content of the book, including the right to do revisions if the publisher requests them. (Paragraph 15)

❏ Require licensees to agree not to add anything to the book, including advertising, without first obtaining the illustrator's consent.

❏ Seek a right of consultation with respect to the price, print run, method of printing, publication date, design, paper, new printings, and similar matters. Most publishers will insist on having the ultimate control over these matters. (Paragraph 15)

❏ Agree to the book's final title, which can only be changed by the agreement of both parties.

❏ Give the illustrator a veto power over material which the publisher wishes to place in the book or on the cover.

❏ Obtain the right to consult regarding the promotional budget, promotional campaign, or distribution of press releases and review copies. (Paragraph 15)

❏ Limit the amount of promotion the publisher can require the illustrator to do.

❏ State that the illustrator shall review proofs or galleys, and give a period of time in which to do this. (Paragraph 15)

❏ Most contracts require authors to pay for authors' alterations once the manuscript is typeset, but this should be only in excess of a percentage of the typesetting cost (such as 15 percent), might be subject to a maximum dollar amount, and should exclude printer's errors or unavoidable updating.

❏ Require that the publisher send out a certain number of review copies to a list of people supplied by the illustrator.

❏ Require the publisher to return the manuscript and all accompanying materials to the illustrator within a certain time period after publication and to give the illustrator page proofs if the illustrator requests them prior to publication. (Paragraph 16)

❏ If valuable materials, such as original art or photographic transparencies, are submitted to the publisher, require that the publisher insure them and be strictly liable for loss or damage.

❏ Provide for the illustrator to receive ten or more free copies of the book and any subsequent editions in a different form, such as a quality paperback after original hardcover publication. (Paragraph 17)

❏ Allow the illustrator to purchase additional copies at a 40 or 50 percent discount from retail price. (Paragraph 17)

❏ Allow the illustrator to sell copies purchased by the illustrator.

❏ If the illustrator wants to sell a large quantity of the book, ask for a discount schedule. For example, 1 to 99 copies might have a 50 percent discount, 100 to 250 copies a 55 percent discount, 251 to 499 copies a 60 percent discount, 500 to 999 copies a 65 percent discount, and 1,000 or more copies a 70 percent or higher discount. If the illustrator can order prior to the publisher's print run, a high discount is even more justifiable.

❏ Require that the publisher pay royalties on copies sold to the illustrator.

❏ The illustrator should have the first option to revise the book at the publisher's request. However, the publisher will expect to have the

❏ right to have the revision done by someone else if the illustrator cannot or will not do it. (Paragraph 18)

❏ If the book may be outdated quickly, state that the publisher must allow a revision within a certain time period, such as two or three years, and that the contract will terminate if the publisher refuses such a revision.

❏ If the illustrator is to do a revision, state that an additional advance shall be negotiated and paid at that time.

❏ If a revision is done by someone else, the cost of this will come from royalties due the illustrator. The cost should only come from royalties payable on the revised book, not the prior edition or other books by the illustrator.

❏ Specify a minimum royalty which the illustrator will receive, even if a revision is done by someone else, or cap how much the royalties can be reduced to pay for the revision.

❏ Give the illustrator the right to remove his or her name from the credits if the revision is not satisfactory.

❏ Make the agreement binding on successors and assigns of the parties. (Paragraph 19)

❏ Do not allow assignment by one party unless the other party consents to this in writing. (Paragraph 19)

❏ Allow the illustrator to assign the right to royalties without obtaining the publisher's consent. (Paragraph 19)

❏ In the event of infringement, state that the parties can sue jointly and, after deducting expenses, share any recovery. If one party chooses not to sue, the other party can sue and, after deducting expenses, share any recovery. (Paragraph 20)

❏ With respect to rights retained by the illustrator, the publisher should have no right to sue for an infringement.

❏ With respect to subsidiary rights in which the illustrator receives more than 50 percent of income, the publisher's right to sue should be limited to the percentage the publisher would receive.

❏ Give the illustrator the right to terminate the contract if the book remains out-of-print after a request by the illustrator that it be put back in print. (Paragraph 21)

❏ Define out-of-print to include when in any 12 months sales are less than 750 copies or royalties are less than a specified amount.

❏ Define out-of-print to mean that the book is not available in bookstores, regardless of whether the publisher has copies.

❏ Define whether a book must be out-of-print in all editions or only those published by the publisher to be deemed out-of-print.

❏ Give the illustrator the right to terminate if the publisher fails to give statements of account, fails to pay, or fails to publish the book. In such cases the illustrator would keep payments received from the publisher. (Paragraph 21)

❏ State that the contract will automatically terminate if the publisher goes bankrupt or becomes insolvent. (Paragraph 21)

❏ If the illustrator fails to deliver a manuscript, the publisher will expect to receive back all payments. (Paragraphs 3 and 21)

❏ If the manuscript delivered in good faith is unsatisfactory to the publisher, the standard publishing contract will require the return of advances but the illustrator can negotiate to retain them. (Paragraph 21)

❏ If possible, avoid any requirement to repay an advance if a book, after rejection by one publisher, is placed with another publisher.

❏ Provide for the reversion of all rights to the illustrator upon termination. (Paragraph 21)

❏ Whatever the ground for termination, the illustrator should have the right to purchase all production materials at scrap value and remaining copies at the lesser of cost or remainder value. (Paragraph 22)

❏ Allow the use of the illustrator's name or picture to promote the work, but require that the promotion be in good taste. (Paragraph 23) The illustrator might seek either to supply the biographical material or have a right of approval over such material.

❏ If the illustrator signs the contract first, a provision might be made to withdraw the offer if the publisher does not sign within thirty or sixty days after receipt of the contract.

❏ The illustrator should resist giving the publisher a security interest in the work, which might entitle the publisher to seize the manuscript and related materials for money owed to the publisher (such as unrecouped advances) under the contract.

❏ If the illustrator has an agent, the contract may provide for payment to the agent. A better approach would be to make the contract subject to the illustrator-agent contract. In any case, the illustrator should have the right to receive direct payment of all monies due other than the agent's commission.

❏ If an agency clause gives the agent a right to act on behalf of the illustrator, review which actions the agent may take.

❏ The illustrator should strike from the contract any provision which limits the creation of competitive works, since this may impair the range of work the illustrator may later create. If the publisher insists on such a provision, the illustrator should narrowly limit its scope with respect to the same subject matter, the same audiences, the same forms of book publication, duration, and geographic extent, and state that such a provision would be enforceable only when the sales of the original book would be impaired.

❏ The publisher may also seek an option for the illustrator's next book. Ideally this will be stricken from the contract. If it is not stricken, it should be an option for one work only on terms to be agreed to (not terms identical to the existing contract). The publisher must accept or reject the work within a limited time period, such as thirty or sixty days, based on an outline (not a complete manuscript).

❏ State that a noncompetition clause or an option clause will be valid only if the publisher is not in breach of the contract and the contract has not been terminated.

❏ Include an arbitration clause. (Paragraph 24)

❏ Review the standard provisions in the introductory pages and compare with Paragraphs 25 to 28.

❏ If there is a joint author, review Form 6.

# Book Publishing Contract

AGREEMENT, entered into as of this _____ day of _____ ____, 19___, between _____ (hereinafter referred to as the "Publisher"), located at _____, and _____ (hereinafter referred to as the "Illustrator"), located at _____.

WHEREAS, the Illustrator wishes to create a book on the subject of _____ (hereinafter referred to as the "Work")

WHEREAS, the Publisher is familiar with the work of the Illustrator and wishes to publish a book by the Illustrator; and

WHEREAS, the parties wish to have said publication performed subject to the mutual obligations, covenants, and conditions herein.

NOW, THEREFORE, in consideration of the foregoing premises and the mutual covenants hereinafter set forth and other valuable considerations, the parties hereto agree as follows:

1. **Grant of Rights.** The Illustrator grants, conveys, and transfers to the Publisher in that unpublished Work titled _____, certain limited, exclusive rights as follows: **(A)** To publish the Work in the form of a _____ book; **(B)** In the territory of _____; **(C)** In the_____ language; and **(D)** For a term of _____ years.

2. **Reservation of Rights.** All rights not specifically granted to the Publisher are reserved to the Illustrator.

3. **Delivery of Manuscript.** On or before the _____ day of _____, 19_____, the Illustrator shall deliver to the Publisher a complete manuscript of approximately _____ words, which shall be reasonably satisfactory in form and content to the Publisher and in conformity with any outline or description attached hereto and made part hereof. The manuscript shall include the additional materials listed in Paragraph 4 (except that if an index is to be provided by the Illustrator, it shall be delivered to the Publisher within thirty days of Illustrator's receipt of paginated galleys). If the Illustrator fails to deliver the complete manuscript within ninety days after receiving notice from the Publisher of failure to deliver on time, the Publisher shall have the right to terminate this Agreement and receive back from the Illustrator all monies advanced to the Illustrator pursuant to Paragraphs 4, 5, and 9. If the Illustrator delivers a manuscript which, after being given detailed instructions for revisions by the Publisher and _____ days to complete such revisions, is not reasonably acceptable to the Publisher, then monies advanced to the Illustrator pursuant to Paragraphs 4, 5, and 9 shall be ❏ retained by the Illustrator ❏ repaid to the Publisher ❏ repaid to the Publisher only in the event the Illustrator subsequently signs a contract with another Publisher for the Work.

4. **Additional Materials.** The following materials shall be provided by the Illustrator _____ _____ _____ _____. The cost of providing these additional materials shall be borne by the Illustrator, provided, however, that the Publisher at the time of signing this Agreement shall give a nonrefundable payment of $_____ to assist the Illustrator in defraying these costs, which payment shall not be deemed an advance to the Illustrator and shall not be recouped as such.

5. **Permissions.** The Illustrator agrees to obtain all permissions that are necessary for the use of materials copyrighted by others. The cost of providing these permissions shall be borne by the Illustrator, provided, however, that the Publisher at the time of signing this Agreement shall give a nonrefundable payment of $_____ to assist the Illustrator in defraying these costs, which payment shall not be deemed an advance to the Illustrator and shall not be recouped as such. Permissions shall be obtained in writing and copies shall be provided to the Publisher when the manuscript is delivered.

**6. Duty to Publish.** The Publisher shall publish the Work within _____ months of the delivery of the complete manuscript. Failure to so publish shall give the Illustrator the right to terminate this Agreement ninety days after giving written notice to the Publisher of the failure to make timely publication. In the event of such termination, the Illustrator shall have no obligation to return monies received pursuant to Paragraphs 4, 5, and 9.

**7. Royalties.** The Publisher shall pay the Illustrator the following royalties: ____ percent of the suggested retail price on the first 5,000 copies sold; ____ percent of the suggested retail price on the next 5,000 copies sold; and ____ percent of the suggested retail price on all copies sold thereafter. These royalty rates shall be discounted only in the following circumstances: _____

_____

All copies sold shall be cumulated for purposes of escalations in the royalty rates, including revised editions, except for editions in a different form (such as a paperback reprint of a hardcover original) which shall be cumulated separately. Copies sold shall be reduced by copies returned in the same royalty category in which the copies were originally reported as sold.

In the event the Publisher has the right pursuant to Paragraph 1(A) to publish the Work in more than one form, the royalty rates specified above shall apply to publication in the form of a _____ book and the royalty rates for other forms shall be specified here: _____

_____

_____

**8. Subsidiary Rights.** The following subsidiary rights may be licensed by the party indicated and the proceeds divided as specified herein:

| Subsidiary Right | Right to License | | Division of Proceeds | |
|---|---|---|---|---|
| | Illustrator | Publisher | Illustrator | Publisher |
| _____ | _____ | _____ | _____ | _____ |
| _____ | _____ | _____ | _____ | _____ |
| _____ | _____ | _____ | _____ | _____ |
| _____ | _____ | _____ | _____ | _____ |
| _____ | _____ | _____ | _____ | _____ |

If the division of proceeds for any subsidiary right changes after the sale of a certain number of copies, indicate which right, the number of copies required to be sold, and the new division of proceeds _____

_____

_____

The Publisher shall have no rights pursuant to this Paragraph 8 if Publisher is in default of any of its obligations under this Agreement. The right to license any subsidiary right not set forth in this Paragraph is retained by the Illustrator. Licensing income shall be divided as specified herein without any reductions for expenses.

Licensing income shall be collected by the party authorized to license the right and the appropriate percentage remitted by that party to the other party within ten days of receipt. Copies of all licenses shall be provided to both parties immediately upon receipt.

**9. Advances.** The Publisher shall, at the time of signing this Agreement, pay to the Illustrator a nonrefundable advance of $_____, which advance shall be recouped by the Publisher from payments due to the Illustrator pursuant to Paragraph 11 of this Agreement.

**10. Accountings.** Commencing as of the date of publication, the Publisher shall report every ____ months to the Illustrator, showing for that period and cumulatively to date the number of copies printed and bound, the number of copies sold and returned for each royalty rate, the number of copies distributed free for publicity purposes, the number of copies remaindered, destroyed, or lost, and the royalties paid to and owed to the Illustrator. If the Publisher sets up a reserve against returns of books, the reserve may only be set up for the four accounting periods following the first publication of the Work and shall in no event exceed 15 percent of royalties due to the Illustrator in any period.

11. **Payments.** The Publisher shall pay the Illustrator all monies due Illustrator pursuant to Paragraph 10 within thirty days of the close of each accounting period.

12. **Right of Inspection.** The Illustrator shall, upon the giving of written notice, have the right to inspect the Publisher's books of account to verify the accountings. If errors in any such accounting are found to be to the Illustrator's disadvantage and represent more than 5 percent of the payment to the Illustrator pursuant to the said accounting, the cost of inspection shall be paid by the Publisher.

13. **Copyright and Authorship Credit.** The Publisher shall, as an express condition of receiving the grant of rights specified in Paragraph 1, take the necessary steps to register the copyright on behalf of the Illustrator and in the Illustrator's name and shall place copyright notice in the Illustrator's name on all copies of the Work. The Illustrator shall receive authorship credit as follows: _____.

14. **Warranty and Indemnity.** The Illustrator warrants and represents that he or she is the sole creator of the Work and owns all rights granted under this Agreement, that the Work is an original creation and has not previously been published (indicate any parts that have been previously published), that the Work does not infringe any other person's copyrights or rights of literary property, nor, to his or her knowledge, does it violate the rights of privacy of, or libel, other persons. The Illustrator agrees to indemnify the Publisher against any final judgment for damages (after all appeals have been exhausted) in any lawsuit based on an actual breach of the foregoing warranties. In addition, the Illustrator shall pay the Publisher's reasonable costs and attorney's fees incurred in defending such a lawsuit, unless the Illustrator chooses to retain his or her own attorney to defend such lawsuit. The Illustrator makes no warranties and shall have no obligation to indemnify the Publisher with respect to materials inserted in the Work at the Publisher's request. Notwithstanding any of the foregoing, in no event shall the Illustrator's liability under this Paragraph exceed $_____ or _____ percent of sums payable to the Illustrator under this Agreement, whichever is the lesser. In the event a lawsuit is brought which may result in the Illustrator having breached his or her warranties under this Paragraph, the Publisher shall have the right to withhold and place in an escrow account _____ percent of sums payable to the Illustrator pursuant to Paragraph 11, but in no event may said withholding exceed the damages alleged in the complaint.

15. **Artistic Control.** The Illustrator and Publisher shall consult with one another with respect to the title of the Work, the price of the Work, the method and means of advertising and selling the Work, the number and destination of free copies, the number of copies to be printed, the method of printing and other publishing processes, the exact date of publication, the form, style, size, type, paper to be used, and like details, how long the plates or film shall be preserved and when they shall be destroyed, and when new printings of the Work shall be made. In the event of disagreement after consultation, the Publisher shall have final power of decision over all the foregoing matters except the following, which shall be controlled by the Illustrator_____ _____. No changes shall be made in the complete manuscript of the Work by persons other than the Illustrator, except for reasonable copy editing, unless the Illustrator consents to such changes. Publisher shall provide the Illustrator with galleys and proofs which the Illustrator shall review and return to the Publisher within thirty (30) days of receipt. If the cost of the Illustrator's alterations (other than for typesetting errors or unavoidable updating) exceeds _____ percent of the cost of the typography, the Publisher shall have the right to deduct such excess from royalties due Illustrator hereunder.

16. **Original Materials.** Within thirty days after publication, the Publisher shall return the original manuscript and all additional materials to the Illustrator. The Publisher shall provide the Illustrator with a copy of the page proofs, if the Illustrator requests them prior to the date of publication.

17. **Free Copies.** The Illustrator shall receive _____ free copies of the Work as published, after which the Illustrator shall have the right to purchase additional copies at a _____ percent discount from the retail price.

**18. Revisions.** The Illustrator agrees to revise the Work on request by the Publisher. If the Illustrator cannot revise the Work or refuses to do so absent good cause, the Publisher shall have the right to have the Work revised by a person competent to do so and shall charge the costs of said revision against payments due the Illustrator under Paragraph 11 for such revised edition. In no event shall such revision costs exceed $ _____ .

**19. Successors and Assigns.** This Agreement may not be assigned by either party wihout the written consent of the other party hereto. The Illustrator, however, shall retain the right to assign payments due hereunder without obtaining the Publisher's consent. This Agreement shall be binding on the parties and their respective heirs, administrators, successors, and assigns.

**20. Infringement.** In the event of an infringement of the rights granted under this Agreement to the Publisher, the Publisher and the Illustrator shall have the right to sue jointly for the infringement and, after deducting the expenses of bringing suit, to share equally in any recovery. If either party chooses not to join in the suit, the other party may proceed and, after deducting all the expenses of bringing the suit, any recovery shall be shared equally between the parties.

**21. Termination.** The Illustrator shall have the right to terminate this Agreement by written notice if: **(A)** the Work goes out-of-print and the Publisher, within ninety days of receiving notice from the Illustrator that the Work is out-of-print, does not place the Work in print again. A work shall be deemed out-of-print if the work is not available for sale in reasonable quantities in normal trade channels; **(B)** if the Publisher fails to provide statements of account pursuant to Paragraph 10; **(C)** if the Publisher fails to make payments pursuant to Paragraphs 4, 5, 9, or 11; or **(D)** if the Publisher fails to publish in a timely manner pursuant to Paragraph 6. The Publisher shall have the right to terminate this Agreement as provided in Paragraph 3. This Agreement shall automatically terminate in the event of the Publisher's insolvency, bankruptcy, or assignment of assets for the benefit of creditors. In the event of termination of the Agreement, the Publisher shall grant, convey, and transfer all rights in the Work back to the Illustrator.

**22. Production Materials and Unbound Copies.** Upon any termination, the Illustrator may, within sixty days of notification of such termination, purchase the plates, offset negatives, or computer drive tapes (if any) at their scrap value and any remaining copies at the lesser of cost or remainder value.

**23. Promotion.** The Illustrator consents to the use of his or her name, portrait, or picture for promotion and advertising of the Work, provided such use is dignified and consistent with the Illustrator's reputation.

**24. Arbitration.** All disputes arising under this Agreement shall be submitted to binding arbitration before _____ _____ in the following location _____ and shall be settled in accordance with the rules of the American Arbitration Association. Judgment upon the arbitration award may be entered in any court having jurisdiction thereof.

**25. Notice.** Where written notice is required hereunder, it may be given by use of first class mail addressed to the Illustrator or Publisher at the addresses given at the beginning of this Agreement and shall be deemed received five days after mailing. Said addresses for notice may be changed by giving written notice of any new address to the other party.

**26. Modifications in Writing.** All modifications of this Agreement must be in writing and signed by both parties.

**27. Waivers and Defaults.** Any waiver of a breach or default hereunder shall not be deemed a waiver of a subsequent breach or default of either the same provision or any other provision of this Agreement.

**28. Governing Law.** This Agreement shall be governed by the laws of _____ State.

IN WITNESS WHEREOF, the parties have signed this Agreement as of the date first set forth above.

Illustrator_____     Publisher_____
                                                               Company Name

                                                By_____
                                                   Authorized Signatory, Title

# Collaboration Contract

**C**ollaboration presents the challenge and reward of blending two or more creative efforts into a single work. For the illustrator this often means creating the visual components of a book while an author writes the text. Publishers offer coauthors a publishing agreement to sign, but a publishing agreement does not resolve the issues likely to arise between the collaborators. That is why a collaboration agreement, such as Form 6, should also be entered into by the illustrator and coauthor. Form 6 deals with an illustrator providing illustrations and an author providing text, but it could easily be modified for a book in which two illustrators each provided art or two authors each provided text. The negotiation checklist, in fact, is a valuable starting point to use for collaborations on other creative projects, such as toys, posters, or games.

The first issue to be resolved is how the copyright in the collaboration will be owned. The copyright law provides that a joint work is "a work prepared by two or more authors with the intention that their contributions be merged into inseparable or interdependent parts of a unitary whole." The collaboration agreement can specify the intention of the parties.

If the copyright is owned jointly, either party can license the work as long as proceeds are equally shared. The collaboration agreement can override this, providing that the parties must agree before licensing the work or indicating that the income will not be equally shared. If one party dies, his or her heirs would inherit the rights in the copyright. Again, the collaboration agreement can alter this by stating that the surviving collaborator will own the entirety of the work and its copyright.

One advantage of a joint work is that the copyright term is the life of the survivor plus 50 years. The term for the collaboration agreement would usually be the same as the term of the copyright.

The responsibilities of the parties must be set out in the greatest detail possible. An outline or synopsis can be attached to the agreement, dividing these responsibilities and giving a schedule for the work.

The division of proceeds from sales of the work must be resolved, especially if the division is not equal or if different types of income will be shared differently. The contract can provide that both parties must agree to any disposition of rights, but it can also specify that one party will control certain rights. For example, the illustrator might want to control licenses of merchandising rights, such as the use of images on apparel, ceramics, or posters, and receive all of the income from such licenses. The agreement should state that the parties are independent of each other and have not formed a partnership, since a partner can legally bind the partnership even if he or she acted outside the authority of the partnership agreement.

The parties must decide how to authorize and share expenses, and what will happen if expenses are incurred but the project is either never completed or never sold. The failure to complete or sell the work raises complicated issues as to how the rights will be treated. It is likely that each party would want to retain the rights in his or her portion of the book and be free to publish that portion by itself or as part of a longer work. Whether this is fair will vary from project to project.

The agreement must determine what will happen if one collaborator fails to complete his or her portion of the work. Likewise, if one collaborator becomes disabled or dies, it is still necessary to complete, market, and revise the work. How will this be done? Probably both artistic and financial control of the project should be given to the active party at this point, rather than involving heirs or other people who were not parties to the original agreement.

The agreement must also deal with how each collaborator will avoid competing with the collaborative work, while not impairing either party's ability to earn a livelihood. For example, can one party create a similar work which might damage the market for the collaborative work? If not, should this be allowed after some period of time? Must the collaborators work together on sequels? Or can each one create his or her own sequels? Any agreement as to future works, whether written negatively as a noncompetition clause or positively as a right to collaborate on sequels, must be approached with the utmost caution. Otherwise the illustrator may find that he or she has agreed to lifelong self-censorship.

If an agent is to be used, the contract should specify who the agent is or, at least, whether both parties must agree to the choice of an agent.

Authorship credit should be specified in the agreement. It is important that the credits accurately reflect what the parties did. The credit could be "by A and B" or "illustrations by A and story by B." "As told to" indicates one person telling their story to another; while "with" suggests that one person did some writing and the other person, usually a professional author, shaped and completed the book. It is against public policy for someone to take credit for writing a book which, in fact, was written by someone else.

The parties will have to give a warranty and indemnity to the publisher. If this clause is breached, both parties will be liable. The collaborators should determine who, in the event of a breach, should pay the publisher: both parties or only the party who created that portion of the work (assuming he or she has sufficient assets to pay for damages and legal fees).

Arbitration may be helpful in collaboration agreements, because certain issues do not lend themselves to determination in advance. For example, should the work be completed if one party is disabled? If it is completed, how should the disabled party's right to share income be affected? Should the nature of the authorship credit change, especially if a third party has been brought in to do substantial work? These and similar questions require a look at what has ac-

tually taken place before a fair result can be obtained.

The collaboration agreement is part of a process which will require the collaborators to contract with yet another party who will market the work. In the case of a book, a publisher will market what the collaborators create. Not only must the collaboration agreement resolve the issues likely to arise between the collaborators, it must also be compatible with reaching agreement with the publisher, who will disseminate the work to its ultimate audience. Form 5, the Book Publishing Contract, is therefore helpful to keep in mind when negotiating Form 6 with a coauthor.

## Filling in the Form

In the Preamble fill in the date and the names and addresses of the parties. In the second Whereas clause the tentative title of the work should be entered. In Paragraph 1 the work should be described and the appropriate boxes checked if a schedule, outline, or synopsis is attached to the agreement. In Paragraph 2 the obligations of each party should be described. In Paragraph 3 fill in the due date. In Paragraph 4 fill in a date for termination if no publishing agreement has been obtained. In Paragraph 5 fill in the first blank if the collaborators choose not to have a jointly owned copyright, and fill in the second blank if the parties choose either not to own jointly certain proprietary rights or not to work together on sequels. In Paragraph 6 provide a dollar limit for expenses for each party. Also in Paragraph 6 show how net proceeds will be divided for publishing and nonpublishing rights, filling in the final blank if certain rights are to be controlled or benefitted from in a way which is an exception to the general approach of the paragraph. Specify the name of any agent in Paragraph 7 and, if there is no agent, check the appropriate box as to whether the parties wish to obtain one. In Paragraph 8 give the credit line and state if the size or color of the names shall ever differ between the collaborators. In Paragraph 9 fill in the blank if one party is not to have artistic control over his or her portion of the work. In Paragraph 13 give the name of an arbitrator and a place for arbitration. In Paragraph 16 specify any limitations on the parties with respect to competitive works. In Paragraph 17 state how recoveries for infringements will be shared. In Paragraph 18 indicate which state's laws will govern the agreement. Have both parties sign.

## Negotiation Checklist

❏ The project should be described in as much detail as possible. If an outline or synopsis exists, it can be attached to the contract. (Paragraph 1)

❏ Indicate precisely and in as much detail as possible the responsibilities of each party. (Paragraph 2)

❏ Specify a due date to complete the work. (Paragraph 3)

❏ If one party fails to complete his or her portion of the work by the due date, consider what should happen and whether there should be an extension, the other party should have the right to complete the work (or hire a third party to complete it), or the rights in each portion of the work should revert to the party creating that portion. (Paragraph 3)

❏ If the work is not completed and each party retains the rights in his or her portion, state that each party is free to do as he or she pleases with that portion.

❏ Specify a work schedule with a sequence of deadlines, so that missing any deadline would have the same consequences as missing the final due date. This may alert one party to difficulties that are developing with his or her

collaborator and give an opportunity to reconcile differences.

❏ If the nature of the collaboration is such that each party will have some portion of work inextricably merged with the portion created by the other party, state whether such merged portions can or cannot be used by either party in the event the work is not completed.

❏ If either party could create a competitive work that would damage the market for the collaborative work, state that for a certain period of time neither party shall create such a work. (See other provisions.)

❏ State that the parties either have a publishing contract or agree to seek such a contract. (Paragraph 4)

❏ Indicate that any publishing contract must be acceptable to both parties, who must each sign it and obey its provisions. (Paragraph 4)

❏ If no publishing contract is obtained by a certain date, allow either party to terminate the contract on written notice to the other party and specify that each party shall keep the rights in the portion of the work that he or she has created. (Paragraph 4)

❏ Require each party to inform the other party regarding any negotiations. (Paragraph 4)

❏ State which party will control the disposition of the various rights, or whether the parties must both agree to any licensing of the work. (Paragraph 4)

❏ If one party negotiates all contracts and licenses, give the other party a veto right and require both parties to sign all documents.

❏ If there are three or more collaborators, state whether licensing, contracts, and artistic decisions will be controlled by one party, a majority vote, or unanimous agreement.

❏ Permit the use of a written power of attorney by one party on behalf of the other in specifically enumerated circumstances.

❏ Require that each collaborator receive an original or, at least, a copy of any contract or license which is entered into. (Paragraph 4)

❏ Specify whether the copyright will be held jointly in the whole work, or whether each party will retain copyright in that portion which he or she has created. (Paragraph 5)

❏ If the copyright is to be jointly owned, state that this will only happen if each party completes his or her portion. (Paragraph 5)

❏ If the copyright is jointly owned, decide whether each party's right in the joint copyright will pass on to heirs in the event of death or become the property of the other party. No provision has to be made if the choice is to have the right be inherited.

❏ If the copyrights are to be separately held by each party, provide for appropriate assignments of rights from each party so rights in the whole work are available for publication and licensing.

❏ If the work creates a trademark, characters, situations, or other rights which might be used later in sequels, determine whether both parties own the trademark or other rights and whether both have the right to do sequels. (Paragraphs 5 and 12)

❏ If both parties have a right to do sequels, consider whether this right shall be limited to a certain number of years after publication (perhaps two to four years) or should expire as of a specific date.

❏ State whether materials created or purchased in the course of developing the books (including research, tapes, interviews, books, equipment, etc.) shall be owned by both parties or by the party which obtained the material. (Paragraph 5)

❏ Specify how the expenses of the parties in creating the project will be shared, especially if the expenses are not shared in the same way income is or if different types of income are shared differently. (Paragraph 6)

❏ If the work is never completed, will one party have to contribute to cover expenses incurred by the other party? (Paragraph 3)

❏ Determine how income, including advances, will be divided. (Paragraph 6)

❏ Specify how advances will be paid back to a publisher if one party fails to complete his or her portion of the work and the entire work cannot be completed. (Paragraph 3)

❏ Determine whether different types of income should be divided differently. For example, should the illustrator share in income from sales of audio cassettes based on readings of the text? Should the writer share in income from merchandising of the illustrations on posters? (Paragraph 6)

❏ If one party arranges the sale of certain rights, should that party receive an extra percentage as a reward?

❏ If one party has several capacities, such as being the illustrator of the original work and the creator of the animation for a film version, should that party be free to receive payment in each capacity?

❏ Specify who will receive money owed and how and when the money will be distributed to the collaborators. Ideally, payment should be direct to each collaborator. (Paragraph 6)

❏ Specify whether money received will be kept in a joint bank account and, if so, whether both parties must sign on that account.

❏ To avoid any conflicts if both parties have agents, determine whether the parties will use an agent, specify the agent if known, and require both parties to sign and obey the contract with the agent. (Paragraph 7)

❏ Specify authorship credit, including the order, size, and color of the names, and the use of the names on promotional or advertising materials. (Paragraph 8)

❏ Determine which party will have artistic control of the work, or whether each party will control his or her own portion. (Paragraph 9)

❏ Specify the conditions under which one party may make or authorize changes in the work of the other party. (Paragraphs 3, 9, and 12)

❏ Require each party to give a warranty and indemnity to the other party, so one party will have some protection against copyright infringements, invasions of privacy, and similar unlawful acts on the part of the other party. (Paragraph 10)

❏ Specify that each party will obtain any releases or licenses to use copyrighted materials in his or her portion of the work and determine how payment will be made for such materials. (Paragraph 10)

❏ Do not allow assignment of the contract, since the duties of an illustrator or author are usually based on personal skills. (Paragraph 11)

❏ Consider carefully whether to allow assignment of money due under the contract, since

a party who has no reward to look forward to may lose interest in the work. (Paragraph 11)

❏ If a party wishes to assign money to become due or any rights in the work, give the other party the first option to purchase this right by matching the best terms offered.

❏ In the event of the death or disability of a party prior to completing the work, decide if the other party should have the right to complete the work. (Paragraph 12)

❏ In the event of death or disability of a party, determine how revisions of the work can be done and how such revisions will be paid for. (Paragraph 12)

❏ If one collaborator dies, decide whether the survivor should control contractual and licensing decisions or whether the estate and heirs should be involved. (Paragraph 12)

❏ In the event of death or disability, create a formula for reallocating the shares of income.

❏ If all collaborators are deceased, provide for the heirs or personal representatives to make financial and artistic decisions. (Paragraph 12)

❏ An arbitration provision is probably wise, because it is usually quicker and less expensive than a court proceeding. (Paragraph 13)

❏ In addition to arbitration, include a mediation provision so that the parties will have an independent mediator seek to resolve disputes before going to arbitration. Unlike arbitration, mediation is not binding on either party.

❏ Specify the agreement's term. (Paragraph 14)

❏ State that the agreement does not create a partnership or joint venture between the parties. (Paragraph 15)

❏ If the promotional or marketing commitment of either party is important to the project, specify what activities that party must undertake.

❏ Have both parties agree to allow the use of their name, portrait, or picture to promote the work.

❏ If the parties agree not to compete with the work, the exact limitations must be specified. (Paragraph 16. See other provisions.)

❏ If the work is infringed by others, determine how to bring suit, share costs, and share any recovery. (Paragraph 17)

❏ Review the standard provisions in the introductory pages and compare to Paragraph 18.

**Other Provisions that can be added to Form 6:**

❏ Exclusivity. This provision is designed for the situation in which a person tells his or her story to an author, so it is not likely to be relevant to an illustrator.

**Exclusivity.** The parties hereto agree that this Agreement is an exclusive agreement in that neither party will enter into any other agreements for books or for magazine articles which will diminish the value of any of the parties' respective rights in this Agreement. The Illustrator acknowledges that the following activities by the Coauthor do not violate the preceding sentence: _____

_____

_____.

Further, the Illustrator agrees that the Coauthor is free to sell the publishing and nonpublishing rights to his or her story if such sales will not diminish the value of the parties' respective rights and do not deal with those as-

pects of the Coauthor's story embodied in the Work, and that all proceeds derived by the Coauthor from the granting of such rights are the sole property of the Coauthor.

❏ Noncompetition. The danger of such a noncompetition clause is that one party or the other may be barred from earning a portion of their livelihood.

**Noncompetition.** The parties agree that for a period of _____ years neither party shall authorize the publication of any other work in book form which directly competes with and would significantly diminish the market for the Work. This noncompetition provision shall not apply in the following circumstances:_____

_____

_____.

# Collaboration Contract

AGREEMENT entered into as of this _____ day of _____, 19___, between _____ (hereinafter referred to as the "Illustrator"), located at _____, and _____ (hereinafter referred to as the "Coauthor"), located at _____.

WHEREAS, each party is familiar with and respects the work of the other; and

WHEREAS, the parties hereto wish to collaborate on a book project tentatively titled _____ _____ (hereinafter referred to as the "Work"); and

WHEREAS, the parties wish to have the creation of the Work governed by the mutual obligations, covenants, and conditions herein;

NOW, THEREFORE, in consideration of the foregoing premises and the mutual covenants hereinafter set forth and other valuable considerations, the parties hereto agree as follows:

1. **Description.** The Work shall be approximately _____ words on the subject of_____ _____ _____ and shall be illustrated by _____ illustrations. Materials other than text and illustrations include _____ _____ _____

   A ❑ schedule ❑ outline ❑ synopsis is attached to and made part of this agreement.

2. **Responsibilities.** The Illustrator shall be responsible for creating approximately _____ illustrations to accompany the text, described more fully as follows:

   Subject_____

   Original Size_____

   Reproduction size_____

   Medium_____

   Number and size of color illustrations_____

   Number and size of black and white illustrations_____

   Other specifications_____

   The Illustrator shall also provide the following materials:_____ _____

   The Coauthor shall be responsible for writing approximately _____ words to serve as the following parts of the text: _____ _____

   The Coauthor shall also provide the following materials:_____ _____

3. **Due Date.** Both Illustrator and Coauthor shall complete their portions of the Work by _____, 19 \_\_\_\_, or by the date for delivery of the manuscript as specified in a publishing contract entered into pursuant to Paragraph 4. If such a publishing contract requires sketches or other materials prior to the date for delivery of the manuscript, the party responsible for same shall provide it to the publisher. In the event either party fails to complete his or her portion of the Work by the due date for reasons other than death or disability, the parties may agree to an extension of the due date or agree to allow a nondefaulting party to complete the Work as if the other party were deceased or disabled. If no agreement can be reached, the arbitrator may award a nondefaulting party the right to complete the Work as if the other party were deceased or disabled or may convey to each party the rights of copyright in that party's completed portion of the Work and specify how the parties shall contribute to any expenses incurred and repay any advances.

4. **Contracts and Licenses.** If a contract for the Work has not already been entered into with a publisher, both Illustrator and Coauthor agree to seek such a contract. Such publishing contract shall be entered into in the names of and signed by both the Illustrator and the Coauthor, each of whom shall comply with and perform all required contractual obligations. If a mutually agreeable publishing contract for initial publication of the Work is not entered into with a Publisher by _____, 19\_\_\_\_, then either party may terminate this agreement by giving written notice to the other party prior to such time as a mutually agreeable publishing contract for initial publication is entered into. Each party shall fully inform the other party of all negotiations for such a publishing contract or with respect to the negotiation of any other licenses or contracts pursuant to this Agreement. The disposition of any right, including the grant of any license, shall require written agreement between both parties hereto. Each party shall receive a copy of any contract, license, or other document relating to this Agreement.

5. **Copyright, Trademarks, and Other Proprietary Rights.** Illustrator and Coauthor agree that the Work shall be copyrighted in both their names, and that upon completion of the Work it is their intention that their respective contributions shall be merged into a joint work with a jointly owned copyright, unless provided to the contrary here:_____. If either party does not complete their portion of the Work, the nature of copyright ownership shall be governed by Paragraph 3. It is further agreed that trademarks, rights in characters, titles, and similar ongoing rights shall be owned by both parties who shall both participate in any sequels under the terms of this Agreement, unless provided to the contrary here:_____. A sequel is defined as a work closely related to the Work in that it is derived from the subject matter of the Work, is similar in style and format to the Work, and is directed toward the same audience as that for the Work. Material of any and all kinds developed or obtained in the course of creating the work shall be ❑ jointly owned ❑ the property of the party who developed or obtained it.

6. **Income and Expenses.** Net proceeds generated by the Work shall be divided as set forth in this Paragraph. Net proceeds are defined as gross proceeds from the sale or license of book rights throughout the world (including but not limited to serializations, condensations, and translations), including advances, minus reasonable expenses. Such expenses shall include agents' fees and the parties' expenses incurred in the creation of the Work, provided that the parties' expenses shall be supported by appropriate verification and shall not exceed $\_\_\_\_ for the Illustrator and $\_\_\_\_ for the Coauthor. Each party shall provide verification for expenses to the other party within ten days of a written request. Unless otherwise provided, the parties' expenses shall be reimbursed from first proceeds received, including but not limited to advances.

   Net proceeds from the sale or license of publishing rights shall be divided \_\_\_\_ percent to the Illustrator and \_\_\_\_ percent to the Coauthor.

Net proceeds from the sale or license of nonpublishing rights in the Work (including but not limited to audio, merchandising, motion picture, stage play, or television rights to the Work), whether such sale or license occurs before or after initial publication of the Work, shall be divided _____ percent to the Illustrator and _____ percent to the Coauthor, unless provided to the contrary here, in which case the following rights shall be treated with respect to division of net proceeds and control or disposition as follows:_____ _____.

If possible, net proceeds shall be paid directly to each party in accordance with the divisions set forth in this Paragraph. If either party is designated to collect such net proceeds, that party shall make immediate payment to the other party of such amounts as are due hereunder.

7. **Agent.** If the parties have entered into an agency agreement with respect to the Work, it is with the following agent:_____. If a contract for the Work has not already been entered into with an agent, both Illustrator and Coauthor agree ❏ to seek such a contract ❏ not to seek such a contract. Any agency contract shall be mutually acceptable to and entered into in the names of and signed by both the Illustrator and the Coauthor, each of whom shall comply with and perform all required contractual obligations.

8. **Authorship Credit.** The credit line for the Work shall be as follows wherever authorship credit is given in the Work or in promotion, advertising, or other ancillary uses:_____ _____. The color and type size for such authorship credit shall be the same for both authors unless provided to the contrary here:_____ _____.

9. **Artistic Control.** Each party shall have artistic control over his or his portion of the Work, unless provided to the contrary here in which case artistic control of the entire Work shall be exercised by _____ _____. The parties shall share ideas and make their work in progress available to the other party for discussion and coordination purposes. Except as provided in Paragraphs 3 and 12, neither party shall at any time make any changes in the portion of the Work created by the other party.

10. **Warranty and Indemnity.** Illustrator and Coauthor each warrant and represent to the other that the respective contributions of each to the Work are original (or that appropriate releases have been obtained and paid for) and do not libel or otherwise violate any right of any person or entity, including but not limited to rights of copyright or privacy. Illustrator and Coauthor each indemnify and hold the other harmless from and against any and all claims, actions, liability, damages, costs, and expenses, including reasonable legal fees and expenses, incurred by the other as a result of the breach of such warranties, representations, and undertakings.

11. **Assignment.** This Agreement shall not be assignable by either party hereto, provided, however, that after completion of the Work, either party may assign the right to receive money pursuant to Paragraph 6 by giving written notice to the other party.

12. **Death or Disability.** In the event that either party dies or suffers a disability that will prevent completion of his or her respective portion of the Work, or of a revision thereof or a sequel thereto, the other party shall have the right to complete that portion or to hire a third party to complete that portion and shall adjust the authorship credit to reflect the revised authorship arrangements. The deceased or disabled party shall receive payments pursuant to Paragraph 6 pro rata to the proportion of his or her work completed or, in the case of a revision or sequel, shall receive payments pursuant to Paragraph 6 after deduction for the cost of revising or creating the sequel with respect to his or her portion of the Work. The active party shall have the sole power to license

and contract with respect to the Work, and approval of the personal representative, heirs, or conservator of the deceased or disabled party shall not be required. If all parties are deceased, the respective heirs or personal representatives shall take the place of the parties for all purposes.

**13. Arbitration.** All disputes arising under this Agreement shall be submitted to binding arbitration before _____ in the following location _____ and shall be settled in accordance with the rules of the American Arbitration Association. Judgment upon the arbitration award may be entered in any court having jurisdiction thereof.

**14. Term.** The term for this Agreement shall be the duration of the copyright, plus any renewals or extensions thereof.

**15. Independent Parties.** The parties to this Agreement are independent of one another, and nothing contained in this Agreement shall make a partnership or joint venture between them.

**16. Competitive Works.** If the parties wish to restrict future activities to avoid competition with the Work, any such restrictions must be stated here: _____

**17. Infringement.** In the event of an infringement of the Work, the Illustrator and Coauthor shall have the right to sue jointly for the infringement and, after deducting the expenses of bringing suit, to share in any recovery as follows:_____. If either party chooses not to join in the suit, the other party may proceed and, after deducting all the expenses of bringing the suit, any recovery shall be shared between the parties as stated in the preceding sentence.

**18. Miscellany.** This Agreement shall be binding upon the parties hereto, their heirs, successors, assigns, and personal representatives. This Agreement constitutes the entire understanding between the parties. Its terms can be modified only by an instrument in writing signed by both parties. Each party shall do all acts and sign all documents required to effectuate this Agreement. A waiver of any breach of any of the provisions of this Agreement shall not be construed as a continuing waiver of other breaches of the same or other provisions hereof. This Agreement shall be governed by the laws of the State of _____.

IN WITNESS WHEREOF, the parties hereto have signed this Agreement as of the date first set forth above.

Illustrator_____     Coauthor_____

# Contract for the Sale of an Artwork

This is a basic contract for the sale of a work of art. A number of provisions, included in the section on other provisions, can be added to Form 7 to govern the relationship of the illustrator to the work after the sale. These provisions are innovative and often approximate the moral rights which protect creators in other nations.

## Filling in the Form

In the Preamble fill in the date and the names and addresses of the parties. In Paragraph 1 describe the work. In Paragraph 3 fill in the price. In Paragraph 5 check the box to indicate who will arrange for delivery and fill in the location and time for delivery and who will pay the expenses for the delivery. In Paragraph 6 fill in when the risk of loss will pass from the illustrator to the collector. In Paragraph 7 fill in the date for the copyright notice. In Paragraph 8 fill in the state whose laws will govern the sale. Both parties should then sign.

## Negotiation Checklist

❏ Make certain title does not pass to the purchaser until the illustrator has been paid in full. (Paragraph 2)

❏ Agree on the price and the payment of sales tax or any other transfer tax. (Paragraph 3)

❏ Agree on the payment of other charges, such as for framing or installation. If the illustrator must travel to install the work, agree on a fee or reimbursement for the travel expenses.

❏ Agree on the time for payment. (Paragraph 4)

❏ If the sale is an installment sale, obtain the right to a security interest in the work. (See the discussion under other provisions.)

❏ Specify the manner of payment, such as by personal check, certified check, cash, credit card, or money order.

❏ Specify the currency for payment. This might be necessary if the collector is foreign or if the illustrator is selling work abroad.

❏ Agree on who arranges and pays for delivery, if the collector can't simply take the work when it is purchased. (Paragraph 5)

❏ Specify a time for delivery. (Paragraph 5)

❏ Agree when the risk of loss or damage to the work passes from the illustrator to the collector. This risk usually passes on delivery, but the time when the risk passes can be altered by contract. If the collector buys the work but leaves it with the illustrator, the risk of loss will not pass to the collector until the collector could reasonably have been expected to pick up the work. The illustrator can avoid the uncertainty of this by providing that the risk of loss passes to the collector at the time of purchase, regardless of whether the work has been delivered. (Paragraph 6)

❏ Agree whether the work will be insured and, if so, by whom. (Paragraph 6.)

❏ Reserve all reproduction rights to the illustrator. (Paragraph 7)

❏ Require copyright notice in the illustrator's name for any reproductions approved by the illustrator. (Paragraph 7)

❏ Review the standard provisions in the introductory pages and compare to Paragraph 8.

**Other Provisions which can be added to Form 7:**

❏ Installment sale. If the illustrator wants to sell the work on an installment basis, the following provision could be added:

**Installment Sale.** The price shall be paid in _____ installments, payable $_____ on _____, 19____; $_____ on _____, 19____; and $_____ on _____, 19____.

❏ Security interest. If the illustrator allows the collector to purchase the work on an installment basis, the illustrator may want the right to have a security interest in the work until payment is made in full. This means that the illustrator would have a right to the work ahead of any of the collector's creditors. Such a provision would state:

**Security Interest.** Collector grants to the Illustrator, and the Illustrator hereby reserves, a security interest under the Uniform Commercial Code in the work and any proceeds derived therefrom until payment is made in full to the Illustrator. Collector agrees to execute and deliver to the Illustrator, in the form requested by the Illustrator, a financing statement and such other documents which the Illustrator may require to perfect its security interest in the work. The Collector agrees not to transfer, pledge, or encumber the work until payment has been made in full, nor to incur any charges or obligations in connection therewith for which the Illustrator may be liable.

To perfect a security interest (which means the formalities have been completed so the illustrator can take precedence over the collector's creditors) requires the filing of Uniform Commercial Code Form 1 with the Secretary of State or local agency for filing such as the County Clerk. Since the collector will usually have to sign what is filed, the contractual provision requires the collector to provide whatever documents the illustrator may need. If large sums are involved or the collector's finances are questionable, these documents might be required at the time of signing the contract of sale.

❏ Nondestruction. The illustrator may want to obligate a collector to return work if the collector no longer wants the work and intends to dispose of it.

**Nondestruction.** The Collector shall not destroy the Work or permit the Work to be destroyed without first offering to return ownership of the Work to the Illustrator or his or her successors in interest.

❏ Integrity and Attribution. This is the heart of the illustrator's moral rights. It gives the illustrator the right to be acknowledged as the creator of his or her work, to have the work be unaltered, and, if the work is altered, to remove the illustrator's name from the work.

**Integrity and Attribution.** The Collector shall not distort, mutilate, or otherwise alter the Work. In the event such distortion, mutilation, or other alteration occurs, whether by action of the Collector or otherwise, the Illustrator shall, in addition to any other rights and remedies, have the right to have his or her name removed from the Work and no longer have it attributed to him or her as its creator.

❏ Right to Exhibit. The illustrator may very well wish to borrow work which has been sold for purposes of exhibition. This provision allows that. It would not be unreasonable to have the right to borrow the work for sixty days every five years.

**Right to Exhibit.** The Illustrator may borrow the Work for up to _____ days once every _____ years for exhibition at a nonprofit institution. The Illustrator shall give the Collector written notice no later than 120 days before the opening and shall provide satisfactory proof of insurance and prepaid transportation. All expenses of the loan to the Illustrator shall be paid for by the Illustrator.

❏ Restoration. The illustrator may want to oversee any restoration to work which has been sold. If the illustrator cannot do the restoration, he or she may nonetheless want the right to consult about the restoration or even approve the restorer.

**Restoration.** In the event of damage to the Work requiring restoration or repair, the Collector shall, if practicable, offer the Illustrator the first opportunity to restore or repair the Work and, in any case, shall consult with the Illustrator with respect to the restoration or repairs.

❏ Resale Proceeds. Following laws which exist in many countries, California enacted an art-resale-proceeds law. This gives an illustrator the right to a part of the proceeds on a profitable sale of his or her art by a subsequent owner. The provision given below seeks to create such a right by contract, but applies only to the first collector to buy the work. To try and bind subsequent owners would require the first collector to agree to include in any contract of sale a provision that the next owner would agree to such a resale proceeds right and also agree to bind the following owner to comply with the provision.

**Resale Proceeds.** On resale or other transfer of the Work for a price or value in excess of that paid in Paragraph 3, the Collector agrees to pay the Illustrator _____ percent of the gross sale price received or, if the Work is transferred other than by sale, to pay _____ percent of the fair market value of the Work as of the date of transfer.

# Contract for the Sale of an Artwork

AGREEMENT made as of the _____ day of _____, 19_____, between _____ (hereinafter referred to as the "Illustrator"), located at _____ _____, and _____ (hereinafter referred to as the "Collector"), located at _____, with respect to the sale of an artwork (hereinafter referred to as the "Work").

WHEREAS, the Illustrator has created the Work and has full right, title, and interest therein; and
WHEREAS, the Illustrator wishes to sell the Work; and
WHEREAS, the Collector has viewed the Work and wishes to purchase it;
NOW, THEREFORE, in consideration of the foregoing premises and the mutual obligations, covenants, and conditions hereinafter set forth, and other valuable considerations, the parties hereto agree as follows:

**1. Description of Work**. The Illustrator describes the Work as follows:

Title: _____

Medium: _____

Size: _____

Framing or Mounting: _____

Year of Creation: _____

Signed by Illustrator:  ❏ Yes   ❏ No

If the Work is part of a limited edition, indicate the method of production _____; the size of the edition_____; how many multiples are signed_____; how many are unsigned_____; how many are numbered_____; how many are unnumbered_____; how many proofs exist_____; the quantity of any prior editions_____; and whether the master image has been cancelled or destroyed  ❏ yes  ❏ no.

**2. Sale.** The Illustrator hereby agrees to sell the Work to the Collector. Title shall pass to the Collector at such time as full payment is received by the Illustrator pursuant to Paragraph 4 hereof.

**3. Price.** The Collector agrees to purchase the Work for the agreed upon price of $_____, and shall also pay any applicable sales or transfer taxes.

**4. Payment**. Payment shall be made in full upon the signing of this Agreement.

**5. Delivery**. The ❏ Illustrator ❏ Collector shall arrange for delivery to the following location:_____ _____ no later than _____, 19____. The expenses of delivery (including, but not limited to, insurance and transportation) shall be paid by _____.

**6. Risk of Loss and Insurance.** The risk of loss or damage to the Work and the provision of any insurance to cover such loss or damage shall be the responsibility of the Collector from the time of_____ _____.

**7. Copyright and Reproduction.** The Illustrator reserves all reproduction rights, including the right to claim statutory copyright, in the Work. The Work may not be photographed, sketched, painted, or reproduced in any manner whatsoever without the express, written consent of the Illustrator. All approved reproductions shall bear the following copyright notice: © by (Illustrator's name) 19____.

**8. Miscellany**. This Agreement shall be binding upon the parties hereto, their heirs, successors, assigns, and personal representatives. This Agreement constitutes the entire understanding between the parties. Its terms can be modified only by an instrument in writing signed by both parties. A waiver of any breach of any of the provisions of this Agreement shall not be construed as a continuing waiver of other breaches of the same or other provisions hereof. This Agreement shall be governed by the laws of the State of _____.

IN WITNESS WHEREOF, the parties hereto have signed this Agreement as of the date first set forth above.

Illustrator _____ Collector _____

# Contract for Receipt and Holding of Artwork

The illustrator frequently faces a dilemma. On the one hand, there is a very good reason to leave art with someone else. On the other hand, this other party has not yet made any commitment to the illustrator. For example, the illustrator may want to leave a portfolio containing original art or hard-to-replace samples with an art director.

Or it may simply be necessary to take art for framing, repairs, or review by a printer prior to undertaking a project. In all of these cases the art is entrusted to someone else.

Once art has left the illustrator's hands, it is important that it be preserved and kept in good condition. Anyone holding the art as part of his or her regular business dealings has a duty of reasonable care. The illustrator may want to raise this standard of care. Insurance may be needed to protect the art.

Another problem that may arise when the illustrator's work is entrusted to someone else is the risk that it may be infringed by unauthorized reproductions or even sold or rented without the illustrator receiving a fee or exercising the right to control what is done with the art. Form 8 makes explicit the restrictions against any such use of the artworks by the party holding them.

The holding fee is designed to encourage that the art not be kept for an unreasonable period of time. Of course, a holding fee may be impractical in many situations (such as when the illustrator is sending the art out for framing or is leaving it with an art director who has not solicited the work for review). Parties entrusted with art may not be willing to agree to a high standard of care or to the insuring of the art. In such cases, the value of Form 8 is that it alerts the illustrator to the risks in giving the art to the other party.

Of course, the illustrator's copyright is protection against unauthorized reproductions and displays. Use of Form 8 alerts the other party to the illustrator's determination to prevent such unauthorized uses.

If the illustrator feels Form 8 will not be agreed to by the other party, a simpler form can be evolved from Form 8. In either case, the recipient should sign the form, if at all possible.

## Filling in the Form

In the Preamble fill in the date and the names and addresses of the parties. In Paragraph 1 give the purpose for which the art has been delivered to the other party. In Paragraph 4 check the boxes to show the duration of recipient's liability and indicate the method of return transportation. In Paragraph 5 check the box regarding insurance. State when the art is to be returned in Paragraph 6 and, if relevant, specify the number of days and holding fee. In Paragraph 7 give the small claims court limit on claims and specify an arbitrator. In Paragraph 8 state which state's laws will govern the agreement. Fill in the Schedule of Artworks with the relevant information (including samples, slides, or other materials, if necessary). Both parties should sign the contract.

## Negotiation Checklist

❑ State the purpose for leaving the artworks with the other party. (Paragraph 1)

❑ Specify that the recipient accepts the information provided on the Schedule of Artworks to show that there is no dispute as to which artworks were delivered and what their values are. (Paragraph 2)

❑ Require immediate, written notification of any dispute as to the listing of artworks or their values. (Paragraph 2)

❑ State that if no objection is made within ten days, the terms shall be considered accepted even if the Recipient has not signed the Form. (Paragraph 2)

❑ Reserve ownership of the physical artworks to the illustrator. (Paragraph 3)

❏ Reserve the copyright and all reproduction rights to the illustrator. (Paragraph 3)

❏ Require that the artworks be held in confidence. (Paragraph 3)

❏ State that the recipient shall be strictly liable in the event of loss, theft, or damage, and indicate the duration of this responsibility. (Paragraph 4)

❏ Require return of the artworks to the illustrator at the recipient's expense. (Paragraph 4)

❏ Require recipient to pay for the transportation from the illustrator to the recipient.

❏ Specify the method of transportation. (Paragraph 4)

❏ Require wall-to-wall all-risks insurance be provided by the recipient. (Paragraph 5)

❏ Make the illustrator a named beneficiary on any insurance policy protecting the artworks.

❏ Provide for the payment of a holding fee to the illustrator if the artworks are kept beyond a certain period of time. (Paragraph 6)

❏ Give the illustrator a security interest in the artworks to protect against claims by creditors of the recipient. Security interests are reviewed under other provisions for Form 7.

❏ State that the illustrator's written permission is required for any reproduction, display, sale, or rental of the artworks. In essence, this requires another contract which would deal specifically with the relevant issues within each arrangement and provide for fees and appropriate limitations. (Paragraph 3)

❏ Compare the standard provisions in the introductory pages with Paragraphs 7-8.

# Contract for Receipt and Holding of Artwork

AGREEMENT entered into as of this _____ day of _____, 19_____, between _____ (hereinafter referred to as the "Illustrator"), located at_____, and _____ (hereinafter referred to as the "Recipient"), located at_____.

WHEREAS, the Illustrator is a professional illustrator of good standing; and

WHEREAS, the Illustrator wishes to leave certain artworks with the Recipient for a limited period of time; and

WHEREAS, the Recipient in the course of its business receives and holds artworks;

NOW, THEREFORE, in consideration of the foregoing premises and the mutual covenants hereinafter set forth and other valuable consideration, the parties hereto agree as follows:

1. **Purpose.** Illustrator hereby agrees to entrust the artworks listed on the Schedule of Artworks to the Recipient for the purpose of: _____

2. **Acceptance.** Recipient accepts the listing and values on the Schedule of Artworks as accurate if not objected to in writing by return mail immediately after receipt of the artworks. If Recipient has not signed this form, any terms on this form not objected to in writing within 10 days shall be deemed accepted.

3. **Ownership and Copyright.** Copyright and all reproduction rights in the artworks, as well as the ownership of the physical artworks themselves, are the property of and reserved to the Illustrator. Recipient acknowledges that the artworks shall be held in confidence and agrees not to display, copy, or modify directly or indirectly any of the artworks submitted, nor will Recipient permit any third party to do any of the foregoing. Reproduction, display, sale, or rental shall be allowed only upon Illustrator's written permission specifying usage and fees.

4. **Loss, Theft, or Damage.** Recipient agrees to assume full responsibility and be strictly liable for loss, theft, or damage to the artworks from the time of ❏ shipment by the Illustrator ❏ receipt by the Recipient until the time of ❏ shipment by the Recipient ❏ receipt by the Illustrator. Recipient further agrees to return all of the artworks at its own expense by the following method of transportation: _____. Reimbursement for loss, theft, or damage to an artwork shall be in the amount of the value entered for that artwork on the Schedule of Artworks. Both Recipient and Illustrator agree that the specified values represent the value of the art.

5. **Insurance.** Recipient ❏ does ❏ does not agree to insure the artworks for all risks from the time of shipment from the artist until the time of delivery to the artist for the values shown on the Schedule of Artworks.

6. **Holding Fees.** The artworks are to be returned to the Illustrator within _____ days after delivery to the Recipient. Each artwork held beyond _____ days from delivery shall incur the following daily holding fee: $_____ which shall be paid to the Illustrator on a weekly basis.

7. **Arbitration.** Recipient and Illustrator agree to submit all disputes hereunder in excess of $_____ to arbitration before _____ at the following location _____ under the rules of the American Arbitration Association. The arbitrator's award shall be final and judgment may be entered on it in any court having jurisdiction thereof.

8. **Miscellany.** This Agreement contains the full understanding between the parties hereto and may only be modified by a written instrument signed by both parties. It shall be governed by the laws of the state of _____.

IN WITNESS WHEREOF, the parties hereto have signed this Agreement as of the date first set forth above.


Illustrator_____     Recipient_____
                                                                        Company Name


                                                 By_____
                                                     Authorized Signatory, Title

## Schedule of Artworks

| | Title | Medium | Description | Framing | Value |
|---|---|---|---|---|---|
| 1. | | | | | |
| 2. | | | | | |
| 3. | | | | | |
| 4. | | | | | |
| 5. | | | | | |
| 6. | | | | | |
| 7. | | | | | |
| 8. | | | | | |
| 9. | | | | | |
| 10. | | | | | |
| 11. | | | | | |
| 12. | | | | | |
| 13. | | | | | |
| 14. | | | | | |
| 15. | | | | | |

# Illustrator—Gallery Contract with Record of Consignment and Statement of Account

**M**any illustrators who sell their work through galleries rely on trust instead of contracts. Trust is fine when everything is going smoothly, but it is of little value after disputes arise and neither party is truly certain which contractual terms originally bound the illustrator and gallery together. Contracts with galleries can vary from a simple consignment of one piece of work to an ongoing representation arrangement, under which the gallery has certain rights to represent more of the illustrator's work.

A basic rule is: never give the gallery rights to sell work that the gallery has no capacity to sell. This means that the scope of the representation must be carefully scrutinized. Also, since the work will be in the possession of the gallery, the issues of damage, loss, and repairs must be resolved.

One danger facing the illustrator is the possibility that the gallery may go bankrupt. If this happens, creditors of the gallery may have a right to seize consigned artwork. Many states have enacted laws to protect the illustrator from such seizures. However, the illustrator must check on a state-by-state basis to determine the status of the law. One way to do this is to contact the nearest group of volunteer lawyers for the arts.

Insofar as possible, the illustrator must verify that the gallery is stable financially. Of course, it can be difficult to know what goes on behind the scenes at an apparently successful enterprise. But late payments to other illustrators or suppliers certainly suggest economic difficulty. In any case, one might want to obtain a security interest in the work in order to have a right to the work even if the gallery does go bankrupt.

One other important issue is the identities of the purchasers of the illustrator's work. If the illustrator does not know who purchased the works and where the purchasers live, a retrospective exhibition and even access to take photographs are nearly impossible. The gallery may resist giving these names on the theory that the illustrator will then sell directly to the gallery's clients. One solution might be to have a neutral third party hold the names and contact the purchasers for reasons specified in the contract, such as a retrospective exhibition.

The commission for the gallery varies in the range of 25 to 50 percent of the retail sale price. Reasons for a higher commission would certainly include higher costs to the gallery in making the sales, such as those incurred in extensive promotion and foreign travel. A related issue is: who will bear the various expenses of exhibitions and promotion? While it is a fair assumption that the gallery will usually carry these expenses, it nonetheless bears review. If the gallery pays for frames or similar items, who will own them after the exhibition?

The illustrator should not be bound for too long a period of time by a contract with a gallery. What was appropriate at one time may no longer serve the illustrator as he or she grows in terms of both aesthetic and financial success. One way to deal with this is to provide for a right of termination after a certain time period, such as one or two years.

Highly successful illustrators may receive a stipend each month from the gallery. This is an amount of money that the illustrator receives regardless of sales. If sales are made, the amounts paid as a stipend are subtracted from the amounts due to the illustrator. Problems can arise when sales are not made and the gallery takes artworks to cover the stipend. If the gallery ends up with too many of the illustrator's works, it is as if the illustrator has an alter ego. The gallery may be tempted to sell its own works by the illustrator ahead of works by the illustrator that are on consignment.

The illustrator may want to create a network with a number of galleries, setting limitations with each as to the types of work, areas, and exclusivity. The mechanism to do this would be a coherent series of contracts that protect the illustrator, while giving the galleries the rights and art that they need to make representing the illustrator remunerative.

The illustrator may also deal with consultants or dealers who do not have galleries. For example, illustrators' reps who sell to corporate America use sales tools such as slides and portfolios, but do not necessarily have galleries. Nonetheless, the same considerations apply to contracts with such representatives as apply to contracts with galleries. Instead of specifying the nature of the exhibition to be given, such a contract might specify the efforts to be made on behalf of the illustrator, or, at least, require best efforts on the part of the representative.

## Filling in the Form

In the Preamble give the date and the names and addresses of the parties. In Paragraph 1 specify whether the agreement is exclusive or nonexclusive, and indicate the geographic area covered, as well as which media will be represented. In Paragraph 2 give the term of the agreement and indicate special grounds for termination, such as the death of a particular employee of the gallery or a change of location by the gallery. In Paragraph 3 indicate how long the illustrator's solo exhibition will be and where the exhibition will take place. Then show how expenses will be shared and who will own any property created from these expenses. In Paragraph 4 give the gallery's commission rate for its own sales as well as the commission rate for the illustrator's sales, if applicable. In Paragraph 7 fill in how often an accounting will be given and when such accountings will commence. In Paragraph 10 specify how much insurance will be provided. In Paragraph 14 give the name of an arbitrator or arbitrating body and fill in the maximum small claims court limit so lawsuits can be brought in small claims court for small amounts. In Paragraph 16 specify which state's laws will govern the agreement. Both parties should sign the agreement. The illustrator should also fill in the Record of Consignment and have a representative of the gallery sign it. The Record of Consignment can be used each

time the illustrator delivers additional works to the gallery. The Statement of Account will be filled out by the gallery when accountings are due (for example, every three months).

## Negotiation Checklist

❏ State that the illustrator is the creator and owner of the consigned artworks and, if required, warrant this to be true.

❏ Determine whether the gallery should have an exclusive or nonexclusive right to represent the illustrator. (Paragraph 1)

❏ Whether the representation is exclusive or nonexclusive, limit the geographical area in which the gallery will represent the illustrator. (Paragraph 1)

❏ Specify the media which the gallery will represent for the illustrator. (Paragraph 1)

❏ If the representation is exclusive, limit the work subject to the contract to that work produced during the term of the contract, not work created before or after the contract. (Paragraph 1)

❏ Require signed documentation of all artwork consigned to the gallery. (Paragraph 1 and the Record of Consignment)

❏ Specify a reasonable term, which should not be too long unless there is also a right to terminate the contract. (Paragraph 2)

❏ Give a right of termination on thirty or sixty days notice to either party. (Paragraph 2)

❏ Provide for termination in the event of the gallery's bankruptcy or insolvency. (Paragraph 2)

❏ Provide for termination if a particular person dies or leaves the employment of the gallery. (Paragraph 2)

❏ Provide for termination in the event of a change of ownership of the gallery.

❏ Provide for termination in the event the gallery moves to a new area. (Paragraph 2)

❏ Provide for termination in the event of a change of the form of ownership of the gallery.

❏ Provide for termination if a specified level of sales is not achieved by the gallery over a certain time period.

❏ Decide whether the death of the illustrator should cause a termination.

❏ In the event of termination, require the gallery to pay the expenses of immediately returning all the consigned artworks to the illustrator. (Paragraph 2)

❏ Require that the gallery keep confidential all transactions on behalf of the illustrator.

❏ Require that the gallery exercise best efforts to sell the illustrator's work.

❏ Specify the efforts to be exercised by the gallery, such as providing an exhibition for a certain number of days during the exhibition season. (Paragraph 3)

❏ Give artistic control over the exhibition and any reproductions of the work to the illustrator. (Paragraph 3)

❏ State that the gallery shall pay all expenses for the exhibition, including the cost of wall-to-wall insurance.

❏ If the gallery will not pay all the expenses of the exhibition, which should be enumerated in any case, determine how the payment of various expenses will be divided between the gallery and the illustrator. (Paragraph 3)

❏ Consider having the gallery pay for the construction of expensive pieces.

❏ Consider having the gallery advance money to pay for construction of expensive pieces. These advances, which should be nonrefundable, would later be recouped by the gallery from sales of the work or by taking ownership of some of the work.

❏ Consider specifying a budget for certain important items, such as promotion, and even detailing how the money will be spent.

❏ State who will own frames and other property created as an expense of the exhibition. (Paragraph 3)

❏ If the illustrator is to provide his or her mailing list to help in the promotion of the exhibition, consider requiring that this list be kept confidential and not be used for other promotional purposes.

❏ Give the commission rate on retail price to be paid to the gallery for each piece sold. (Paragraph 4)

❏ Do not agree to a "net price" commission, under which the gallery agrees to pay a fixed amount to the illustrator when the work is sold, since this will allow the gallery to charge higher prices and, in effect, pay a lower commission rate.

❏ If the gallery is selling works in different media, consider whether the commission should vary from one medium to another.

❏ If sales are substantial, review whether the commission rate should decrease as the volume of sales increases.

❏ If the gallery gives a discount on certain sales, try to have the discount deducted from the gallery's commission rather than shared between the gallery and the illustrators. (Paragraph 4)

❏ If the representation is exclusive as to area or types of work, decide if the illustrator must pay a commission to the gallery on sales by the illustrator. If so, which types of sales will be covered and how much will the commission be. It should certainly be less than what the gallery would receive from sales due to the gallery's own efforts. (Paragraph 4)

❏ If the illustrator is to pay a commission on certain sales by the illustrator, exclude transfers by gift or barter from such a requirement.

❏ If the illustrator is to pay a commission on certain sales by the illustrator, consider excluding a certain dollar amount of sales from this requirement.

❏ If the gallery will sell through other galleries, resolve the issue of double commissions.

❏ Specify the retail prices and allowable discounts for sales of the work. (Paragraph 5 and the Record of Consignment)

❏ Require that the gallery pay the illustrator as soon as possible after sale. (Paragraph 6)

❏ Require the illustrator's consent to sales on approval or credit. Sales on approval basically involve loaning the work to a collector who has agreed to purchase the work if he or she approves of it after the loan period. This may also be in the form of a sale with a right to return the work during a specified period of time, in which case payment might not be made in full until that time period had elapsed. (Paragraph 6)

❏ Have the gallery guarantee sales on credit.

❏ Have first proceeds from sales on approval or credit paid to the illustrator. (Paragraph 6)

❏ Consider having the gallery purchase work outright, instead of taking it on consignment.

❏ Consider asking for a stipend, an amount paid every month regardless of sales, which would

be nonrefundable and paid back by sales of art to the gallery if amounts due the illustrator from sales to collectors were insufficient. (See other provisions.)

❏ If the gallery is buying work outright, or is paying a stipend which may result in the gallery buying work, consider specifying the price at which the work must be sold. State that the artist shall receive a part of the resale proceeds if the work is sold for a higher price.

❏ Require periodic accountings by the gallery which include all the information the illustrator needs to know that the payment is correct and where the art is. (Paragraph 7 and Statement of Account)

❏ Require a final accounting upon termination of the agreement. (Paragraph 8)

❏ Make the gallery strictly responsible for loss or damage from the receipt of the work until it is returned to the illustrator. (Paragraph 9)

❏ If possible, have the gallery arrange shipment from the illustrator to the gallery and make the gallery responsible for loss or damage during that time period.

❏ Provide that in the event of loss or damage that cannot be restored, the illustrator shall receive the same monies that would be due if the work had been sold. (Paragraph 9)

❏ Give the illustrator control over any restoration of work. (Paragraph 9)

❏ Require the gallery to insure the work for a portion of the retail price, presumably enough to pay the illustrator in full in the event of loss or damage. (Paragraph 10)

❏ Make the illustrator a named beneficiary of the gallery's insurance policy with respect to the illustrator's work and provide proof of this insurance to the illustrator.

❏ Review which risks are covered by any insurance and which risks may be excluded, such as loss by mysterious disappearance or damage due to frequent handling.

❏ Give the illustrator a security interest to protect the work from creditors of the gallery and require the gallery to execute any documents necessary to perfect the security interest. Security interests are reviewed in the discussion of Form 7. (Paragraph 12)

❏ Require the gallery to post a sign stating that the illustrator's work is on consignment, since this will protect the work from creditors of the gallery.

❏ Provide for title to pass from the illustrator directly to any purchaser and, if that purchaser is the gallery, only after full payment has been received by the illustrator. (Paragraph 12)

❏ Have the gallery agree not to encumber the consigned art in any way for which the illustrator may be liable. (Paragraph 12)

❏ Review the standard provisions in the introductory pages and compare with Paragraphs 13-16.

❏ Keep in mind that state laws vary greatly with respect to illustrator-gallery relationships, so the choice of which state's law will govern may be far more important than is the case in most contracts. (Paragraph 16)

### Other Provisions that can be added to Form 7:

❏ Stipend. The regular flow of income to the illustrator can be very important. This is what a stipend provides, whether it is paid on a weekly, monthly, or other periodic basis. Such a stipend should always be stated to be nonrefundable. However, the stipend must still be repaid, either by reducing sums payable to the illustrator from sales, or by having the gallery purchase work from the illustrator. A somewhat less sophisticated approach would be to have the gallery simply pay one sum as an advance against future sales. Such an advance usually would be paid on signing the contract. If the gallery is purchasing art to pay back an advance or stipend, it will only credit the illustrator with what the illustrator would have received had the art been sold (not the full retail price, since the gallery's commission would have been subtracted from that). The following provision is one approach to a contract with a stipend:

**Stipend.** The Gallery shall pay the Illustrator the nonrefundable sums of $_____ monthly, commencing with the first payment on the signing of this Agreement and continuing with payments on the first day of each month for the term of this Agreement. All funds paid the Illustrator hereunder shall be deemed advances which are to be recouped by the Gallery as follows: (1) By subtracting such advances from sums due the Illustrator for sales of art under this Agreement; or (2) In the event sums due the Illustrator do not equal or exceed such advances, by purchasing a sufficient number of consigned artworks that sums due the Illustrator equal or exceed such advances. If the Gallery is purchasing artworks hereunder, the Illustrator shall be credited for the amount which the Illustrator would have received had the work been sold by the Gallery to an outside purchaser at the retail price specified in the Record of Consignment.

❏ Best Efforts. The requirement that the gallery use best efforts is hard to make into a legal issue, since best efforts is a rather subjective term. It is really better to try and specify exactly what the gallery is required to do. However, there may be some value to include a best efforts provision such as the following:

**Best Efforts.** The Gallery shall use its best efforts to fulfill its obligations pursuant to this Agreement.

# Illustrator—Gallery Contract with Record of Consignment and Statement of Account

AGREEMENT entered into as of this _____ day of _____, 19_____, between_____ (hereinafter referred to as the "Illustrator"), located at _____, and _____ (hereinafter referred to as the "Gallery"), located at _____.

WHEREAS, the Illustrator is a professional illustrator of good standing; and

WHEREAS, the Illustrator wishes to have certain artworks represented by the Gallery, and

WHEREAS, the Gallery wishes to represent the Illustrator under the terms and conditions of this Agreement,

NOW, THEREFORE, in consideration of the foregoing premises and the mutual covenants hereinafter set forth and other valuable consideration, the parties hereto agree as follows:

1. **Scope of Agency.** The Illustrator appoints the Gallery to act as Illustrator's ❏ exclusive ❏ nonexclusive agent in the following geographic area:_____ for the exhibition and sales of artworks in the following media: _____. This agency shall cover only artwork completed by the Illustrator while this Agreement is in force. The Gallery shall document receipt of all works consigned hereunder by signing and returning to the Illustrator a Record of Consignment in the form annexed to this contract as Appendix A.

2. **Term and Termination.** This Agreement shall have a term of _____ years and may be terminated by either party giving sixty days written notice to the other party. The Agreement shall automatically terminate with the death of the Illustrator, the death or termination of employment of _____ with the Gallery, if the Gallery moves outside of the area of _____, or if the Gallery becomes bankrupt or insolvent. On termination, all works consigned hereunder shall immediately be returned to the Illustrator at the expense of the Gallery.

3. **Exhibitions.** The Gallery shall provide a solo exhibition for the Illustrator of _____ days between _____ and _____ in the exhibition space located at _____ which shall be exclusively devoted to the Illustrator's exhibition for the specified time period. The Illustrator shall have artistic control over the exhibition of his or her work and the quality of reproduction of such work for promotional or advertising purposes. The expenses of the exhibition shall be paid for in the respective percentages shown below:

| Exhibition Expenses | Illustrator | Gallery |
|---|---|---|
| Transporting work to gallery (including insurance and packing).............. | _____ | _____ |
| Advertising.......................................................................... | _____ | _____ |
| Catalogs............................................................................. | _____ | _____ |
| Announcements.................................................................... | _____ | _____ |
| Frames............................................................................... | _____ | _____ |
| Special installations............................................................. | _____ | _____ |
| Photographing work.............................................................. | _____ | _____ |
| Party for opening.................................................................. | _____ | _____ |
| Shipping to purchasers.......................................................... | _____ | _____ |
| Transporting work back to illustrator (including insurance and packing) | _____ | _____ |
| All other expenses arising from the exhibition................................ | _____ | _____ |

No expense which is to be shared shall be incurred by either party without the prior written consent of the other party as to the amount of the expense. After the exhibition, the frames, photographs, negatives, and any other tangible property created in the course of the exhibition shall be the property of _____.

4. **Commissions**. The Gallery shall receive a commission of ____ percent of the retail price of each work sold. In the case of discount sales, the discount shall be deducted from the Gallery's commission. If the Gallery's agency is exclusive, then the Gallery shall receive a commission of _____ percent of the retail price for each studio sale by the Illustrator that falls within the scope of the Gallery's exclusivity. Works done on a commissioned basis by the Illustrator ❑ shall ❑ shall not be considered studio sales on which the Gallery may be entitled to a commission.

5. **Prices**. The Gallery shall sell the works at the retail prices shown on the Record of Consignment, subject to the Gallery's right to make customary trade discounts to such purchasers as museums and designers.

6. **Payments**. The Gallery shall pay the Illustrator all proceeds due to the Illustrator within thirty days of sale. No sales on approval or credit shall be made without the Illustrator's written consent and, in such cases, the first proceeds received by the Gallery shall be paid to the Illustrator until the Illustrator has been paid all proceeds due.

7. **Accounting**. The Gallery shall furnish the Illustrator with an accounting every _____ months in the form attached hereto as Appendix B, the first such accounting to be given on the first day of _____, 19____. Each accounting shall state for each work sold during the accounting period the following information: the title of the work, the date of sale, the sale price, the name and address of the purchaser, the amounts due the Gallery and the Illustrator, and the location of all works consigned to the Gallery that have not been sold. An accounting shall be provided in the event of termination of this Agreement.

8. **Inspection of Books.** The Gallery shall maintain accurate books and documentation with respect to all transactions entered into for the Illustrator. On the Illustrator's written request, the Gallery will permit the Illustrator or the Illustrator's authorized representative to examine these books and documentation during normal business hours of the Gallery.

9. **Loss or Damage.** The Gallery shall be responsible for the safekeeping of all consigned artworks. The Gallery shall be strictly liable for loss or damage to any consigned artwork from the date of delivery to the Gallery until the work is returned to the Illustrator or delivered to a purchaser. In the event of loss or damage that cannot be restored, the Illustrator shall receive the same amount as if the work had been sold at the retail price listed in the Record of Consignment. If restoration is undertaken, the Illustrator shall have a veto power over the choice of the restorer.

10. **Insurance.** The Gallery shall insure the work for ____ percent of the retail price shown in the Record of Consignment.

11. **Copyright.** The Gallery shall take all steps necessary to insure that the Illustrator's copyright in the consigned works is protected, including but not limited to requiring copyright notices on all reproductions of the works used for any purpose whatsoever.

12. **Security Interest.** Title to and a security interest in any works consigned or proceeds of sale under this Agreement are reserved to the Illustrator. In the event of any default by the Gallery, the Illustrator shall have all the rights of a secured party under the Uniform Commercial Code and the works shall not be subject to claims by the Gallery's creditors. The Gallery agrees to execute and deliver to the Illustrator, in the form requested by the Illustrator, a financing statement and such other documents which the Illustrator may require to perfect its security interest in the works. In the event of the purchase of any work by a party other than the Gallery, title shall pass directly from the Illustrator to the other party. In the event of the purchase of any work by the Gallery, title

shall pass only upon full payment to the Illustrator of all sums due hereunder. The Gallery agrees not to pledge or encumber any works in its possession, nor to incur any charge or obligation in connection therewith for which the Illustrator may be liable.

**13. Assignment.** This Agreement shall not be assignable by either party hereto, provided, however, that the Illustrator shall have the right to assign money due him or her hereunder.

**14. Arbitration.** All disputes arising under this Agreement shall be submitted to binding arbitration before _____ in the following location _____ and the arbitration award may be entered for judgement in any court having jurisdiction thereof. Notwithstanding the foregoing, either party may refuse to arbitrate when the dispute is for a sum of less than $_____.

**15. Modifications.** All modifications of this Agreement must be in writing and signed by both parties. This Agreement constitutes the entire understanding between the parties hereto.

**16. Governing Law.** This Agreement shall be governed by the laws of the State of _____.

IN WITNESS WHEREOF, the parties hereto have signed this Agreement as of the date first set forth above.

Illustrator_____     Gallery_____
                                                                      Company Name

                                                By_____
                                                        Authorized Signatory, Title

**APPENDIX A:    Record of Consignment**

This is to acknowledge receipt of the following works of art on consignment:

| | Title | Medium | Description | Retail Price |
|---|---|---|---|---|
| 1. | | | | |
| 2. | | | | |
| 3. | | | | |
| 4. | | | | |
| 5. | | | | |
| 6. | | | | |
| 7. | | | | |
| 8. | | | | |
| 9. | | | | |

Gallery _____
                          Company Name

By _____
            Authorized Signatory, Title

**APPENDIX B:    Statement of Account**

Date: _____, 19_____

Acounting for Period from _____, 19_____, through _____, 19_____.

The following works were sold during this period:

| Title | Date Sold | Purchaser's Name and Address | Sale Price | Gallery's Commission | Due Illustrator |
|---|---|---|---|---|---|
| 1._____ | ____ | _____ | _____ | _____ | _____ |
| _____ | ____ | _____ | _____ | _____ | _____ |
| 2._____ | ____ | _____ | _____ | _____ | _____ |
| _____ | ____ | _____ | _____ | _____ | _____ |
| 3._____ | ____ | _____ | _____ | _____ | _____ |
| _____ | ____ | _____ | _____ | _____ | _____ |
| 4._____ | ____ | _____ | _____ | _____ | _____ |
| _____ | ____ | _____ | _____ | _____ | _____ |

The total due you of $_____ is enclosed with this Statement of Account.

The following works remain on consignment with the gallery:

| Title | Location |
|---|---|
| 1._____ | _____ |
| 2._____ | _____ |
| 3._____ | _____ |
| 4._____ | _____ |
| 5._____ | _____ |
| 6._____ | _____ |
| 7._____ | _____ |
| 8._____ | _____ |
| 9._____ | _____ |

Gallery _____
Company Name

By _____
Authorized Signatory, Title

# Illustrator's Lecture Contract

**M**any illustrators find lecturing to be an important source of income as well as a rewarding opportunity to express their feelings about their art and being an illustrator. High schools, colleges, museums, art societies, and other institutions often invite illustrators to lecture. Slides of the art may be used during these lectures and, in some cases, an exhibition may be mounted during the illustrator's visit.

A contract ensures that everything goes smoothly. For example, who should pay for slides that the illustrator has to make for that particular lecture? Who will pay for transportation to and from the lecture? Who will supply materials for a demonstration of technique? Will the illustrator have to give one lecture in a day or, as the institution might prefer, many more? Will the illustrator have to review portfolios of students? Resolving these kinds of questions, as well as the amount of and time to pay the fee, will make any lecture a more rewarding experience.

## Filling in the Form

In the Preamble give the date and the names and addresses of the parties. In Paragraph 1 give the dates when the illustrator will lecture, the nature and extent of the services the illustrator will perform, and the form in which the illustrator is to bring examples of his or her work. In Paragraph 2 specify the fee to be paid to the illustrator and when it will be paid during the illustrator's visit. In Paragraph 3 give the amounts of expenses to be paid (or state that none or all of these expenses are to be paid), specify which expenses other than travel and food and lodging are covered, and show what will be provided by the sponsor, such as food or lodging. In Paragraph 5 state the interest rate for late payments. In Paragraph 10 give which state's law will govern the contract. Then have both parties sign the contract. In the Schedule of Artworks list the artworks to be brought to the lecture and their insurance value.

## Negotiation Checklist

❑ How long will the illustrator have to stay at the sponsoring institution in order to perform the required services? (Paragraph 1)

❑ What are the nature and extent of the services that the illustrator will have to perform? (Paragraph 1)

❑ What slides, original art, or other materials must the illustrator bring? (Paragraph 1)

❑ Specify the work facilities which the sponsor will provide the illustrator. (Paragraph 2)

❑ Specify the fee to be paid to the illustrator. (Paragraph 2)

❑ Give a time for payment of the fee. (Paragraph 2)

❑ Consider having part of the fee paid in advance.

❑ Specify the expenses which will be paid by the sponsor, including the time for payment of these expenses. (Paragraph 3)

❑ Indicate what the sponsor may provide in place of paying expenses, such as giving lodging, meals, or a car. (Paragraph 3)

❑ If illness prevents the illustrator from coming to lecture, state that an effort will be made to find another date. (Paragraph 4)

❑ If the sponsor must cancel for a reason beyond its control, indicate that the expenses incurred by the illustrator must be paid and that an attempt will be made to reschedule. (Paragraph 4)

❏ If the sponsor cancels within 48 hours of the time illustrator is to arrive, consider requiring the full fee as well as expenses be paid.

❏ Provide for the payment of interest on late payments by the sponsor. (Paragraph 5)

❏ Retain for the illustrator all rights, including copyrights, in any recordings of any kind which may be made of the illustrator's visit. (Paragraph 6)

❏ If the sponsor wishes to use a recording of the illustrator's visit, such as a video, require that the sponsor obtain the illustrator's written permission and that, if appropriate, a fee be negotiated for this use. (Paragraph 6)

❏ State that the sponsor is strictly responsible for loss or damage to any artworks from the time they leave the illustrator's studio until they are returned there. (Paragraph 7)

❏ Require the sponsor to insure artworks and specify the values for insurance. (Paragraph 7)

❏ Consider which risks may be excluded from the insurance coverage.

❏ Consider whether the illustrator should be the beneficiary of the insurance coverage of his or her works.

❏ State who will pay the cost of packing and shipping the works to and from the sponsor. (Paragraph 8)

❏ Indicate who will take the responsibility to pack and ship the works to and from the sponsor.

❏ Compare the standard provisions in the introductory pages with Paragraphs 9-10.

# Illustrator's Lecture Contract

AGREEMENT, dated the _____ day of _____, 19 _____, between_____ (hereinafter referred to as the "Illustrator"), located at _____and _____(hereinafter referred to as the "Sponsor"), located at _____.

WHEREAS, the Sponsor is familiar with and admires the work of the Illustrator; and

WHEREAS, the Sponsor wishes the Illustrator to visit the Sponsor to enhance the opportunities for its students to have contact with working professional illustrator; and

WHEREAS, the Illustrator wishes to lecture with respect to his or her work and perform such other services as this contract may call for;

NOW, THEREFORE, in consideration of the foregoing premises and the mutual covenants hereinafter set forth and other valuable considerations, the parties hereto agree as follows:

1. **Illustrator to Lecture.** The Illustrator hereby agrees to come to the Sponsor on the following date(s):_____ _____ and perform the following services: _____.

   The Illustrator shall use best efforts to make his or her services as productive as possible to the Sponsor. The Illustrator further agrees to bring examples of his or her own work in the form of _____ _____.

2. **Payment.** The Sponsor agrees to pay as full compensation for the Illustrator's services rendered under Paragraph 1 the sum of $_____. This sum shall be payable to the Illustrator on completion of the _____ day of the Illustrator's residence with the Sponsor.

3. **Expenses.** In addition to the payments provided under Paragraph 2, the Sponsor agrees to reimburse the Illustrator for the following expenses:

   **(A)** Travel expenses in the amount of $_____.

   **(B)** Food and lodging expenses in the amount of $_____.

   **(C)** Other expenses listed here:_____in the amount of $_____.

   The reimbursement for travel expenses shall be made fourteen (14 days prior to the earliest date specified in Paragraph 1). The reimbursement for food, lodging, and other expenses shall be made at the date of payment specified in Paragraph 2, unless a contrary date is specified here:_____.

   In addition, the Sponsor shall provide the Illustrator with the following:

   **(A)** Tickets for travel, rental car, or other modes of transportation as follows: _____ _____

   **(B)** Food and lodging as follows: _____ _____

   **(C)** Other hospitality as follows: _____ _____

4. **Inability to Perform.** If the Illustrator is unable to appear on the dates scheduled in Paragraph 1 due to illness, the Sponsor shall have no obligation to make any payments under Paragraphs 2 and 3, but shall attempt to reschedule the Illustrator's appearance at a mutually acceptable future date. If the Sponsor is prevented from

having the Illustrator appear by Acts of God, hurricane, flood, governmental order, or other cause beyond its control, the Sponsor shall be responsible only for the payment of such expenses under Paragraph 3 as the Illustrator shall have actually incurred. The Sponsor agrees in such a case to attempt to reschedule the Illustrator's appearance at a mutually acceptable future date.

5. **Late Payment.** The Sponsor agrees that, in the event it is late in making payment of amounts due to the Illustrator under Paragraphs 2, 3, or 8, it will pay as additional liquidated damages _____ percent in interest on the amounts it is owing to the Author, said interest to run from the date stipulated for payment in Paragraphs 2, 3, or 8 until such time as payment is made.

6. **Copyrights and Recordings.** Both parties agree that the Illustrator shall retain all rights, including copyrights, in relation to recordings of any kind made of the appearance or any works shown in the course thereof. The term "recording" as used herein shall include any recording made by electrical transcription, tape recording, wire recording, film, videotape, or other similar or dissimilar method of recording, whether now known or hereinafter developed. No use of any such recording shall be made by the Sponsor without the written consent of the Author and, if stipulated therein, additional compensation for such use.

7. **Insurance and Loss or Damage.** The sponsor agrees that it shall provide wall-to-wall insurance for the works listed on the Schedule of Art Works for the values specified therein. The Sponsor agrees that it shall be fully responsible and have strict liability for any loss or damage to the artwork from the time said artwork leaves the Illustrator's residence or studio until such time as it is returned there.

8. **Packing and Shipping.** The Sponsor agrees that it shall fully bear any costs of packing and shipping necessary to deliver the works specified in Paragraph 7 to the Sponsor and return them to the Illustrator's residence or studio.

9. **Modification.** This contract contains the full understanding between the parties hereto and may only be modified in a written instrument signed by both parties.

10. **Governing Law.** This contract shall be governed by the laws of the State of _____.

IN WITNESS WHEREOF, the parties hereto have signed this Agreement as of the date first set forth above.

Author_____     Sponsor_____
                                                                            Company Name

                                             By_____
                                                             Authorized Signatory, Title

**Schedule of Artworks**

| | Title | Medium | Size | Value |
|---|---|---|---|---|
| 1. | | | | |
| 2. | | | | |
| 3. | | | | |
| 4. | | | | |
| 5. | | | | |
| 6. | | | | |
| 7. | | | | |

# Licensing Contract to Merchandise Images

**L**icensing is the granting of rights to use images created by the illustrator on posters, calendars, greeting cards and stationery, apparel, wall paper, mugs and other household items, or any of innumerable other applications. Needless to say, this can be very lucrative for the illustrator. So many of the products used in everyday life depend on visual qualities to make them attractive to purchasers. These qualities may reside in the design of the product itself or in the use of images on the product. For the illustrator to enter the world of manufactured, mass-produced goods necessitates appropriate business arrangements.

The best guide for illustrators on the subject of licensing is *Licensing Art & Design* by Caryn Leland (Allworth Press, distributed by North Light Books). The potentially large sums of money involved, as well as the possible complexity of licensing agreements, make *Licensing Art & Design* a valuable resource for illustrators who either are licensing images or would like to enter the field of licensing.

Form 11, the Licensing Contract to Merchandise Images, is adapted from a short-form licensing agreement which appears in *Licensing Art & Design.*

## Filling in the Form

In the Preamble fill in the date and the names and addresses of the parties. In Paragraph 1 indicate whether the rights are exclusive or nonexclusive, give the name and description of the image, state what types of merchandise the image can be used for, specify the geographical area for distribution, and limit the term of the distribution. In Paragraph 3 specify the advance, if any, and the royalty percentage. State the date on which payments and statements of account are to begin in Paragraph 4. Indicate the number of samples to be given to the illustrator in Paragraph 6. In Paragraph 13 specify which state's laws will govern the contract. Give addresses for correspondence relating to the contract in Paragraph 14. Have both parties sign the contract.

## Negotiation Checklist

❏ Carefully describe the image to be licensed. (Paragraph 1)

❏ State whether the rights given to the licensee are exclusive or nonexclusive. (Paragraph 1)

❏ Indicate which kinds of merchandise the image is being licensed for. (Paragraph 1)

❏ State the area in which the licensee may sell the licensed products. (Paragraph 1)

❏ Give a term for the licensing contract. (Paragraph 1)

❏ Reserve all copyrights in the image to the illustrator. (Paragraph 2)

❏ Require that credit and copyright notice in the illustrator's name appear on all licensed products. (Paragraph 2)

❏ Require that credit and copyright notice in the illustrator's name appear on packaging, advertising, displays, and all publicity.

❏ Have the right to approve packaging, advertising, displays, and publicity.

❏ Give the licensee the right to use the artist's name and, in an appropriate case, picture, provided that any use must be to promote the product using the image and must be dignified.

❏ Determine whether the royalty should be based on retail price or, as is more commonly the case, on net price (which is what the manufacturer receives). (Paragraph 3)

❏ If any expenses are to reduce the amount upon which royalties are calculated, these expenses must be specified. (Paragraph 3)

❏ Specify the royalty percentage. (Paragraph 3)

❏ Require the licensee to pay an advance against royalties to be earned. (Paragraph 3)

❏ Indicate that any advance is nonrefundable. (Paragraph 3)

❏ Require minimum royalty payments for the term of the contract, regardless of sales.

❏ Require monthly or quarterly statements of account, accompanied by any payments which are due. (Paragraph 4)

❏ Specify the information to be contained in the statement of account, such as units sold, total revenues received, special discounts, and the like. (Paragraph 4)

❏ Give the illustrator a right to inspect the books and records of the licensee. (Paragraph 5)

❏ If an inspection of the books and records uncovers an error to the disadvantage of the illustrator, and that error is more than 5 percent of the amount owed the illustrator, then require the licensee to pay for the cost of the inspection and any related costs.

❏ Provide for a certain number of samples to be given to the illustrator by the manufacturer. (Paragraph 6)

❏ Give the illustrator a right to purchase additional samples at manufacturing cost or, at least, at no more than the price paid by wholesalers. (Paragraph 6)

❏ Consider whether the illustrator will want the right to sell the products at retail price, rather than being restricted to using the samples and other units purchased for personal use.

❏ Give the illustrator a right of approval over the quality of the reproductions in order to protect the illustrator's reputation. (Paragraph 7)

❏ Require that the licensee use best efforts to promote the licensed products. (Paragraph 8)

❏ Specify the amount of money that the licensee must spend on promotion.

❏ Specify the type of promotion that the licensee will provide.

❏ Reserve all rights to the illustrator which are not expressly transferred to the licensee. (Paragraph 9)

❏ If the licensee's usage may create trademark or other rights in the product, it is important that these rights be owned by the illustrator after termination of the license.

❏ Require the licensee to indemnify the illustrator for any costs arising out of the use of the image on the licensed products. (Paragraph 10)

❏ Have the licensee provide liability insurance, with the illustrator as a named beneficiary, to protect against defects in the licensed products.

❏ Forbid assignment by the licensee, but let the illustrator assign royalties. (Paragraph 11)

❏ Specify the grounds for terminating the contract, such as the bankruptcy or insolvency of the licensee, failure of the licensee to obey the terms of the contract, cessation of manufacture of the product, or insufficent sales of the licensed products. (This is partially covered in Paragraph 4.)

❏ Compare the standard provisions in the introductory pages with Paragraphs 12-15.

# Licensing Contract to Merchandise Images

AGREEMENT made this _____ day of _____, 19_____, between _____ (hereinafter referred to as the "Illustrator"), located at _____ and _____ (hereinafter referred to as the "Licensee"), located at _____ with respect to the use of a certain image created by the Illustrator (hereinafter referred to as the "Image") for manufactured products (hereinafter referred to as the "Licensed Products").

WHEREAS, the Illustrator is a professional illustrator of good standing; and

WHEREAS, the Illustrator has created the Image which the Illustrator wishes to license for purposes of manufacture and sale; and

WHEREAS, the Licensee wishes to use the Image to create a certain product or products for manufacture and sale; and

WHEREAS, both parties want to achieve the best possible quality to generate maximum sales;

NOW, THEREFORE, in consideration of the foregoing premises and the mutual covenants hereinafter set forth and other valuable consideration, the parties hereto agree as follows:

1. **Grant of Merchandising Rights.** The Illustrator grants to the Licensee the ❏ exclusive ❏ nonexclusive right to use the Image, titled _____ and described as _____, which was created and is owned by the Illustrator, as or as part of the following type(s) of merchandise:_____ _____ for manufacture, distribution, and sale by the Licensee in the following geographical area:_____ _____ and for the following period of time: _____.

2. **Ownership of Copyright.** The Illustrator shall retain all copyrights in and to the Image. The Licensee shall identify the Illustrator as the creator of the Image on the Licensed Products and shall reproduce thereon a copyright notice for the Illustrator which shall include the word "Copyright" or the symbol for copyright, the Illustrator's name, and the year date of first publication.

3. **Advance and Royalties.** Licensee agrees to pay Illustrator a nonrefundable advance in the amount of $_____ upon signing this Agreement, which advance shall be recouped from first royalties due hereunder. Licensee further agrees to pay Illustrator a royalty of _____ ( _____ %) percent of the net sales of the Licensed Products. "Net Sales" as used herein shall mean sales to customers less prepaid freight and credits for lawful and customary volume rebates, actual returns, and allowances. Royalties shall be deemed to accrue when the Licensed Products are sold, shipped, or invoiced, whichever first occurs.

4. **Payments and Statements of Account.** Royalty payments shall be paid monthly on the first day of each month commencing _____, 19 _____, and Licensee shall with each payment furnish Illustrator with a monthly statement of account showing the kinds and quantities of all Licensed Products sold, the prices received therefor, and all deductions for freight, volume rebates, returns, and allowances. The Illustrator shall have the right to terminate this Agreement upon thirty (30) days notice if Licensee fails to make any payment required of it and does not cure this default within said thirty (30) days, whereupon all rights granted herein shall revert immediately to the Illustrator.

5. **Inspection of Books and Records.** Illustrator shall have the right to inspect Licensee's books and records concerning sales of the Licensed Products upon prior written notice.

**6. Samples.** Licensee shall give the Illustrator _____ samples of the Licensed Products for the Illustrator's personal use. The Illustrator shall have the right to purchase additional samples of the Licensed Products at the Licensee's manufacturing cost.

**7. Quality of Reproductions.** The Illustrator shall have the right to approve the quality of the reproduction of the Image on the Licensed Products, and the Illustrator agrees not to withhold approval unreasonably.

**8. Promotion.** Licensee shall use its best efforts to promote, distribute, and sell the Licensed Products.

**9. Reservation of Rights.** All rights not specifically transferred by this Agreement are reserved to the Illustrator.

**10. Indemnification.** The Licensee shall hold the Illustrator harmless from and against any loss, expense, or damage occasioned by any claim, demand, suit, or recovery against the Illustrator arising out of the use of the Image for the Licensed Products.

**11. Assignment.** Neither party shall assign rights or obligations under this Agreement, except that the Illustrator may assign the right to receive money due hereunder.

**12. Nature of Contract.** Nothing herein shall be construed to constitute the parties hereto joint venturers, nor shall any similar relationship be deemed to exist between them.

**13. Governing Law.** This Agreement shall be construed in accordance with the laws of _____; Licensee consents to the jurisdiction of the courts of _____.

**14. Addresses.** All notices, demands, payments, royalty payments, and statements shall be sent to the Illustrator at the following address _____ and to the Licensee at _____.

**15. Modifications in Writing.** This Agreement constitutes the entire agreement between the parties hereto and shall not be modified, amended, or changed in any way except by a written agreement signed by both parties hereto.

IN WITNESS WHEREOF, the parties have signed this Agreement as of the date first set forth above.

Illustrator_____     Licensee_____
                                                                Company Name


                                                 By_____
                                                        Authorized Signatory, Title

# Release Form for Models

Illustrators often portray people in their art. Because of this, illustrators must be aware of individual's rights to privacy and publicity. While the intricacies of these laws can be reviewed in *Legal Guide for the Visual Artist*, this summary will help alert the illustrator to potential dangers.

The right to privacy can take a number of forms. For example, state laws and court decisions forbid the use of a person's name, portrait, or picture for purposes of advertising or trade. This raises the question of the definitions for the terms "advertising" and "trade." Public display of an image which showed or implied something embarrassing and untrue about someone would also constitute a violation of the right to privacy. And physically intruding into a private space such as a home or office, perhaps to take a photograph for use as a reference, could be an invasion of privacy.

The right of publicity is the right which a celebrity creates in his or her name, image, and voice. To use the celebrity's image for commercial gain violates this right of publicity. And, while the right of privacy generally protects only living people, a number of states have enacted laws to protect the publicity rights of celebrities even after death. These state laws supplement court decisions which held that celebrities who exploited the commercial value of their names and images while alive had publicity rights after death.

On the other hand, use of people's images for newsworthy and editorial purposes is protected by the First Amendment. No releases need be obtained for such uses, which serve the public interest.

What should the illustrator do about all this? The wisest course is to obtain a model release from anyone who will be recognizable in an artwork, including people who can be recognized from parts of their body other than the face. Even if showing the art in a gallery or museum might not create a privacy issue, there is always the possibility that an image will be reproduced in other ways. For example, the image from a painting can be used for posters, postcards, and T-shirts, all of which are clearly trade uses. Or that image can be used in an advertisement. Only by having a model release can the illustrator ensure the right to exploit the commercial value of the image in the future.

Form 12 allows the illustrator (and others who obtain the illustrator's permission) to use the model's image for advertising and trade. While some states may not require written releases or the payment of money for a release, it is always wise to use a written release and make at least a small payment as consideration. By the way, Form 12 is intended for use with friends and acquaintances who pose, as well as with professional models.

It is also important to be aware that if the release is intended to cover one use, and the image is then used in a distorted and embarrassing way for a different purpose, the release may not protect the illustrator, regardless of what it says. For example: a model signed a model release for a bookstore's advertisement, in which she was to appear in bed reading a book. This advertisement was later changed and used by a bedsheet manufacturer known for its salacious advertisements. The title on the book became pornographic and a leering old man was placed next to the bed looking at the model. This invaded the model's privacy despite her having signed a release.

In general, a minor must have a parent or guardian give consent. While the illustrator should check the law in his or her state, the age of majority in most states is eighteen.

The illustrator should be certain to have the release signed during the session, since it is easy to forget if left for signing later. Also, releases should be kept systematically so that each one can be related to the artwork in which its signatory appears. A simple numbering system can be used to connect the releases to the artworks. While a witness isn't a necessity, having one can help if a question is later raised about the validity of the release.

If the illustrator is asked to use a release form supplied by someone else, the illustrator must make certain that the form protects the illustrator. The negotiation checklist will be helpful in reviewing the provided form and suggesting changes to strengthen the form.

## Filling in the Form

Fill in the dollar amount being paid as consideration for the release. Then fill in the name of the model and the name of the illustrator. Have the model and a witness sign the form. Obtain the addresses for both the model and the witness and date the form. If the model is a minor, have the parent or guardian sign. Have the witness sign and give the addresses of the witness and the parent or guardian as well as the date.

## Negotiation Checklist

❏ Be certain that some amount of money, even a token amount, is actually paid as consideration for the release.

❏ Have the release given not only to the illustrator, but also to the illustrator's estate and anyone else the illustrator might want to assign rights to (such as a manufacturer of posters or T-shirts).

❏ State that the grant is irrevocable.

❏ Cover the use of the name as well as the image of the person.

❏ Include the right to use the image in all forms, media, and manners of use.

❏ Include the right to make distorted or changed versions of the image as well as composite images.

❏ Allow advertising and trade uses.

❏ Allow any other lawful use.

❏ Have the model waive any right to review the finished artwork, including written copy to accompany the artwork.

❏ Have the model recite that he or she is of full age.

❏ If the model is a minor, have a parent or guardian sign the release.

# Release Form for Models

In consideration of _____ Dollars ($_____), receipt of which is acknowledged, I, _____, do hereby give _____, his or her assigns, licensees, and legal representatives the irrevocable right to use my name (or any fictional name), picture, portrait, or photograph in all forms and media and in all manners, including composite or distorted representations, for advertising, trade, or any other lawful purposes, and I waive any right to inspect or approve the finished version(s), including written copy that may be created in connection therewith. I am of full age.* I have read this release and am fully familiar with its contents.

Witness_____     Model_____

Address_____     Address_____

Date _____, 19 ___

**Consent (if applicable)**

I am the parent or guardian of the minor named above and have the legal authority to execute the above release. I approve the foregoing and waive any rights in the premises.

Witness_____     Parent or Guardian_____

Address_____     Address_____

Date _____, 19 ___

* Delete this sentence if the subject is a minor. The parent or guardian must then sign the consent.

# Property Release

**P**roperty does not have rights of privacy or publicity. A public building, a horse running in a field, and a bowl of fruit are all freely available to be portrayed in art.

Nonetheless, there may be times when the illustrator will want to obtain a release for the use of property belonging to others. This might include personal property, such as jewelry or clothing, or the interiors of private buildings (especially if admission is charged). The most important reason for the release is to have a contract that details the terms of use of the property.

If the illustrator is lent property to use in a commissioned work, and has any intention of using that artwork in some way other than the commission, a release should be obtained. For example, if an illustrator were hired to do a portrait of a pet, selling that portrait to a manufacturer of dog food for use as product packaging would be a breach of an implied provision of the contract. Such a use would require the owner's permission, which could be obtained by using Form 13.

If the owner could be identified from the property, especially if the owner might be embarrassed in some way by the association with the artwork, it is wise to have a property release.

As with releases for models, property releases should be signed at the time the property is used, and payment, even if only a token payment, should be made to the owner of the property.

## Filling in the Form

Fill in the amount being paid for use of the property, as well as the name and address of the owner and the name of the illustrator. Then specify the property which will be used. Finally, have both parties sign the release, obtain a witness to each signature (if possible), and give the date.

## Negotiation Checklist

❑ Make some payment, however small, as consideration for the release.

❑ Be certain the release runs in favor of the illustrator's assigns and estate as well as the illustrator.

❑ State that the release is irrevocable.

❑ Include the right to copyright and publish the image made from the property.

❑ Include the right to use the image in all forms, media, and manners of use.

❑ Permit advertising and trade uses.

❑ Allow any other lawful use.

❑ State that the owner has full and sole authority to give the release.

❑ Retain the right to make distorted or changed versions of the image as well as composite images.

❑ Allow use of the owner's name or a fictional name in connection with the image of the property.

❑ Permit color or black and white images, as well as any type of derivative work.

❑ Have the owner waive any right to review the finished artwork, including written copy to accompany the artwork.

❑ Make certain the owner is of full age and has the capacity to give the release.

# Property Release

In consideration of the sum of _____Dollars ($_____),

receipt of which is hereby acknowledged, I, _____,

located at _____, do irrevocably authorize

_____, his or her assigns, licensees, heirs, and legal representatives, to copyright, publish, and use in all forms and media and in all manners for advertising, trade, or any other lawful purpose, images of the following property which I own and have full and sole authority to license for such uses: _____ _____,

regardless of whether said use is composite or distorted in character or form, whether said use is made in conjunction with my own name or with a fictitious name, or whether said use is made in color or otherwise or other derivative works are made through any medium.

I waive any right that I may have to inspect or approve the finished version(s), including written copy that may be used in connection therewith.

I am of full age and have every right to contract in my own name with respect to the foregoing matters. I have read the above authorization and release prior to its execution and I am fully cognizant of its contents.

Witness_____        Owner_____

Address_____        Date _____, 19____

# Permission Form

**M**any projects require obtaining permission from the owners of copyrighted materials such as photographs, paintings, articles, or books. The illustrator ignores obtaining such permissions at great peril. Not only is it unethical to use someone else's work without permission, it can also lead to liability for copyright infringement and breach of contract.

Of course, some copyrighted works have entered the public domain, which means that they can be freely copied by anyone. For works published by United States authors on or before December 31, 1977, the maximum term of copyright protection was 75 years. If such a work is more than 75 years old, it should be in the public domain in the United States (but may have a different term of protection in other countries).

For works published on or after January 1, 1978, the term of protection is usually the life of the author plus 50 years, so these works would only be in the public domain if copyright notice had been omitted or improper. This complicated topic is discussed fully in *Legal Guide for the Visual Artist*. The absence of a copyright notice on works published between January 1, 1978 and February 28, 1989 (when the United States joined the Berne Copyright Union) does not necessarily mean the work entered the public domain. On or after March 1, 1989, copyright notice is no longer required to preserve copyright protection, although such notice does confer some benefits under the copyright law. A basic rule would be to obtain permission for any work published on or after January 1, 1978, unless the illustrator is certain the work is in the public domain.

Fair use offers another way in which the illustrator may avoid having to obtain a permission, even though the work is protected by a valid copyright. The copyright law states that copying "for purposes such as criticism, comment, news reporting, teaching (including multiple copies for classroom use), scholarship, or research, is not an infringement of copyright." To evaluate whether a use is a fair use depends on four factors set forth in the law: "(1) the purpose and character of the use, including whether such use is of a commercial nature or is for nonprofit educational purposes; (2) the nature of the copyrighted work; (3) the amount and substantiality of the portion used...and (4) the effect of the use upon the potential market for or value of the copyrighted work." These guidelines have to be applied on a case-by-case basis. If there is any doubt, it is best to seek permission to use the work.

One obstacle to obtaining permissions is locating the person who owns the rights. A good starting point, of course, is to contact the publisher of the material, since the publisher may have the right to grant permissions. If the author's address is available, the author can be contacted directly. In some cases, permissions may have to be obtained from more than one party. Authors' societies and agents may be helpful in tracking down the owners of rights.

For an hourly fee, the Copyright Office will search its records to aid in establishing the copyright status of a work. Copyright Office Circular R22, "How to Investigate the Copyright Status of a Work," explains more fully what the Copyright Office can and cannot do. Circulars and forms can be ordered from the Copyright Office by calling (202) 707-9100.

Obtaining permissions can be time-consuming, so starting early in a project is wise. A log should be kept of each request for a permission. In the log, each request is given a number. The log describes the material to be used, lists the name and address of the owner of the rights, shows when the request was made and when any reply was received, indicates if a fee must be paid, and includes any special conditions required by the owner.

Fees may very well have to be paid for certain permissions. The standard book publishing agreement does not provide for the publisher to pay these fees, although the illustrator can negotiate for such a contribution. Also, publisher's agreements usually make the illustrator liable if lawsuits develop for permissions which should have been obtained by the illustrator. In any case, the illustrator should keep in mind that permission fees are negotiable and vary widely in amount. For a project that will require many permissions, advance research as to the amount of the fees is a necessity.

## Filling in the Form

The form should be accompanied by a cover letter requesting that two copies of the form be signed and one copy returned. The name and address of the illustrator, the title of the illustrator's book, and the name of the illustrator's publisher, should be filled in. Then the nature of the material should be specified, such as text, photograph, illustration, poem, and so on. The source should be described along with an exact description of the material. If available, fill in the date of publication, the publisher, and the author. Any copyright notice or credit line to accompany the material should be shown. State after other provisions any special limitations on the rights granted and also indicate the amount of any fee to be paid. If all the rights are not controlled by the person giving the permission, then that person will have to indicate who else to contact. If more than one person must approve the permission, make certain there are enough signature lines. If the rights are owned by a corporation, add the company name and the title of the authorized signatory. A stamped, self-addressed envelope and a photocopy of the material to be used might make a speedy response more likely.

## Negotiation Checklist

❑ State that the permission extends not only to the illustrator, but also to the illustrator's successors and assigns. Certainly the permission must extend to the illustrator's publisher.

❑ Describe the material to be used carefully, including a photocopy if that would help.

❑ Obtain the right to use the material in future editions and revisions of the book, as well as in the present edition.

❑ State that nonexclusive world rights in all languages are being granted.

❑ In an unusual situation, seek exclusivity for certain uses of the material. This form does not seek exclusivity.

❑ Negotiate a fee, if requested. Whether a fee is appropriate, and its amount, will depend on whether the project is likely to earn a substantial return.

❑ If a fee is paid, add a provision requiring the party giving the permission to warrant that the material does not violate any copyright or other rights and to indemnify the illustrator against any losses caused if the warranty is incorrect.

❑ Keep a log on all correspondence relating to permission forms and be certain one copy of each signed permission has been returned for the illustrator's files.

# Permission Form

The Undersigned hereby grant(s) permission to _____ (hereinafter

referred to as the "Illustrator"), located at _____ ,

and to the Illustrator's successors and assigns, to use the material specified in this Permission Form in the book

titled _____ to be

published by _____ .

This permission is for the following material:

Nature of material _____

Source _____

Exact description of material, including page numbers_____

If published, date of publication _____

Publisher _____

Author(s) _____

This material may be used in the Illustrator's book and in any future revisions and editions thereof, including nonex-clusive world rights in all languages.

It is understood that the grant of this permission shall in no way restrict republication of the material by the Under-signed or others authorized by the Undersigned.

If specified here, the material shall be accompanied on publication by a copyright notice as follows_____

_____

and a credit line as follows _____ .

Other provisions, if any: _____

If specified here, the requested rights are not controlled in their entirety by the Undersigned and the following owners must be contacted: _____

_____

One copy of this Permission Form shall be returned to the Illustrator and one copy shall be retained by the Under-signed.

_____          _____
Authorized Signatory                                      Date

_____          _____
Authorized Signatory                                      Date

# Nondisclosure Agreement for Submitting Ideas

**W**hat can be more frustrating than having a great idea and not being able to share it with anyone? If the idea has commercial value, sharing it is often the first step on the way to realizing the remunerative potential of the concept. The illustrator wants to show the idea to a publisher, manufacturer, or producer. But how can the idea be protected?

Ideas are not protected by copyright, because copyright only protects the concrete expression of an idea. The idea to sketch the White House is not copyrightable, while a sketch of the White House certainly is protected by copyright. The idea to have a television series in which each program would have an artist teach illustration by sketching a well-known landmark in his or her locale is not copyrightable, but each program would be protected by copyright. Of course, copyright is not the only form of legal protection. An idea might be patentable or lead to the creation of a trademark, but such cases are less likely and certainly require expert legal assistance. How does an illustrator disclose an idea for an image, a format, a product, or other creations without risking that the listener, or potential business associate, will simply steal the idea?

This can be done by the creation of an express contract, an implied contract (revealed by the course of dealing between the parties), or a fiduciary relationship (in which one party owes a duty of trust to the other party). Form 15, the Nondisclosure Agreement, creates an express contract between the party disclosing the idea and the party receiving it. Form 15 is adapted from a letter agreement in *Licensing Art & Design* by Caryn Leland (Allworth Press, distributed by North Light Books).

What should be done if a company refuses to sign a nondisclosure agreement or, even worse, has its own agreement for the illustrator to sign? Such an agreement might say that the company will not be liable for using a similar idea and will probably place a maximum value on the idea (such as a few hundred dollars). At this point, the illustrator has to evaluate the risk. Does the company have a good reputation or is it notorious for appropriating ideas? Are there other companies, which could be approached with the idea, that would be willing to sign a nondisclosure agreement? If not, taking the risk may make more sense than never exploiting the idea at all. A number of steps, set out in the negotiation checklist, should then be taken to try and gain some protection. The illustrator will have to make these evaluations on a case-by-case basis.

## Filling in the Form

In the Preamble fill in the date and the names and addresses of the parties. In Paragraph 1 describe the information to be disclosed without giving away what it is. Have both parties sign the agreement.

## Negotiation Checklist

❑ Disclose what the information concerns without giving away what is new or innovative. For example, "an idea for a new format for a series to teach illustration" might interest a producer but would not give away the particulars of the idea (i.e., using different illustrators teaching at landmarks in different locales). (Paragraph 1)

❑ State that the recipient is reviewing the information to decide whether to embark on commercial exploitation. (Paragraph 2)

❑ Require the recipient to agree not to use or transfer the information. (Paragraph 3)

❑ State that the recipient receives no rights in the information. (Paragraph 3)

❑ Require the recipient to keep the information confidential. (Paragraph 4)

❑ State that the recipient acknowledges that disclosure of the information would cause irreparable harm to the illustrator. (Paragraph 4)

❑ Require good faith negotiations if the recipient wishes to use the information after disclosure. (Paragraph 5)

❑ Allow no use of the information unless agreement is reached after such good faith negotiations. (Paragraph 5)

If the illustrator wishes to disclose the information despite the other party's refusal to sign the illustrator's nondisclosure form, the illustrator should take a number of steps:

❑ First, before submission, the idea should be sent to a neutral third party (such as a notary public or professional arts society) to be held in confidence.

❑ Anything submitted should be marked with copyright and trademark notices, when appropriate. For example, the idea may not be copyrightable, but the written explanation of the idea certainly is. The copyright notice could be for that explanation, but might make the recipient more hesitant to steal the idea.

❑ If an appointment is made, confirm it by letter in advance and sign any log for visitors.

❑ After any meeting, send a letter that covers what happened at the meeting (including any disclosure of confidential information and any assurances that information will be kept confidential) and, if at all possible, have any proposal or followup from the recipient be in writing.

# Nondisclosure Agreement for Submitting Ideas

AGREEMENT, entered into as of this _____ day of _____, 19___, between_____ (hereinafter referred to as the "Illustrator"), located at _____, and _____ (hereinafter referred to as the "Recipient"), located at _____.

WHEREAS, the Illustrator has developed certain valuable information, concepts, ideas, or designs, which the Illustrator deems confidential (hereinafter referred to as the "Information"); and

WHEREAS, the Recipient is in the business of using such Information for its projects and wishes to review the Information; and

WHEREAS, the Illustrator wishes to disclose this Information to the Recipient; and

WHEREAS, the Recipient is willing not to disclose this Information, as provided in this Agreement.

NOW, THEREFORE, in consideration of the foregoing premises and the mutual covenants hereinafter set forth and other valuable considerations, the parties hereto agree as follows:

1.  **Disclosure.** Illustrator shall disclose to the Recipient the Information, which concerns:_____
    _____

2.  **Purpose.** Recipient agrees that this disclosure is only for the purpose of the Recipient's evaluation to determine its interest in the commercial exploitation of the Information.

3.  **Limitation on Use.** Recipient agrees not to manufacture, sell, deal in, or otherwise use or appropriate the disclosed Information in any way whatsoever, including but not limited to adaptation, imitation, redesign, or modification. Nothing contained in this Agreement shall be deemed to give Recipient any rights whatsoever in and to the Information.

4.  **Confidentiality.** Recipient understands and agrees that the unauthorized disclosure of the Information by the Recipient to others would irreparably damage the Illustrator. As consideration and in return for the disclosure of this Information, the Recipient shall keep secret and hold in confidence all such Information and treat the Information as if it were the Recipient's own proprietary property by not disclosing it to any person or entity.

5.  **Good Faith Negotiations.** If, on the basis of the evaluation of the Information, Recipient wishes to pursue the exploitation thereof, Recipient agrees to enter into good faith negotiations to arrive at a mutually satisfactory agreement for these purposes. Until and unless such an agreement is entered into, this nondisclosure Agreement shall remain in force.

6.  **Miscellany.** This Agreement shall be binding upon and shall inure to the benefit of the parties and their respective legal representatives, successors, and assigns.

IN WITNESS WHEREOF, the parties have signed this Agreement as of the date first set forth above.

Illustrator_____     Recipient_____
                                                            Company Name

                                                  By_____
                                                            Authorized Signatory, Title

# Copyright Transfer Form

The copyright law defines a transfer of copyright as an assignment "of a copyright or of any of the exclusive rights comprised in a copyright, whether or not it is limited in time or place of effect, but not including a nonexclusive license." A transfer is, in some way, exclusive. The person receiving a transfer has a right to do what no one else can do. For example, the transfer might be of the right to make copies of the work in the form of posters for distribution in the United States for a period of one year. While this transfer is far less than all rights in the copyright, it is nonetheless exclusive within its time and place of effect.

Any transfer of an exclusive right must be in writing, and signed either by the owner of the rights being conveyed or by the owner's authorized agent. While not necessary to make the assignment valid, notarization of the signature is *prima facie* proof that the assignment was signed by the owner or agent.

Form 16 can be used in a variety of situations. If the illustrator wanted to receive back rights which had been transferred in the past, the illustrator could take an all-rights transfer. If the illustrator enters into a contract involving the transfer of an exclusive right, the parties may not want to reveal all the financial data and other terms contained in the contract. Form 16 could then be used as a short form to be executed along with the contract for the purpose of recordation in the Copyright Office. The assignment in Form 16 should conform exactly to the assignment in the contract itself.

Recordation of copyright transfers with the Copyright Office can be quite important. Any transfer should be recorded within thirty days if executed in the United States, or within sixty days if executed outside the United States. Otherwise, a later conflicting transfer, if recorded first and taken in good faith without knowledge of the earlier transfer, will prevail over the earlier transfer. Simply put, if the same exclusive rights are sold twice and the first buyer doesn't record the transfer, it is quite possible that the second buyer who does record the transfer will be found to own the rights.

Any document relating to a copyright, whether a transfer of an exclusive right or only a nonexclusive license, can be recorded with the Copyright Office. Such recordation gives constructive notice to the world about the facts in the document recorded. Constructive notice means that a person will be held to have knowledge of the document even if, in fact, he or she did not know about it. Recordation gives constructive notice only if (1) the document (or supporting materials) identifies the work to which it pertains so that the recorded document would be revealed by a reasonable search under the title or registration number of the work, and (2) registration has been made for the work.

Another good reason to record exclusive transfers is that a nonexclusive license, whether recorded or not, can have priority over a conflicting exclusive transfer. If the nonexclusive license is written and signed and was taken before the execution of the transfer or taken in good faith before recordation of the transfer and without notice of the transfer, it will prevail over the transfer.

A fee must be paid to record documents. Once paid, the Register of Copyrights will record the document and return a certificate of recordation.

## Filling in the Form

Give the name and address of the party giving the assignment (the assignor) and the name and address of the party receiving the assignment. Specify the rights transferred. Describe the work or works by title, registration number, and the nature of the work. Date the transfer and have the assignor sign it. If the assignor is a corporation, use a corporate form for the signature.

## Negotiation Checklist

❏ Be certain that consideration (something of value, whether a promise or money) is actually given to the assignor.

❏ Have the transfer benefit the successors in interest of the assignee.

❏ If the illustrator is making the transfer, limit the rights transferred as narrowly as possible.

❏ Describe the works as completely as possible, including title, registration number, and the nature of the work.

❏ Have the assignor or the authorized agent of the assignor sign the assignment.

❏ Notarize the assignment so that the signature will be presumed valid.

❏ If the assignment is to the illustrator, such as an assignment back to the illustrator of rights previously conveyed, an all-rights provision can be used. (See other provisions)

**Other Provisions that can be added to Form 16:**

❏ Rights transferred. When indicating the rights transferred, the following provision could be used if the illustrator is to receive all rights. Obviously, the illustrator should avoid giving such a transfer to another party.

**Rights Transferred.** All right, title, and interest, including any statutory copyright together with the right to secure renewals and extensions of such copyright throughout the world, for the full term of said copyright or statutory copyright and any renewal or extension of same that is or may be granted throughout the world.

# Copyright Transfer Form

FOR VALUABLE CONSIDERATION, the receipt of which is hereby acknowledged, _____
(hereinafter referred to as the "Assignor"), located at _____,
does hereby transfer and assign to _____, located
at _____, his or her heirs, executors, administrators,
and assigns, the following rights: _____
_____ in the copyrights
in the works described as follows:

| Title | Registration Number | Nature of Work |
|---|---|---|
| _____ | _____ | _____ |
| _____ | _____ | _____ |
| _____ | _____ | _____ |
| _____ | _____ | _____ |
| _____ | _____ | _____ |

IN WITNESS WHEREOF, the Assignor has executed this instrument on the _____ day of _____, 19____.


Assignor_____

# Application for Copyright Registration of an Artwork

To register an artwork, the illustrator must send a completed Form VA, a nonrefundable filing fee, and a nonreturnable deposit portraying the artwork to be registered. These three items should be sent together to the Register of Copyrights, Copyright Office, Library of Congress, Washington, D.C. 20559.

The instructions for filling in Form VA are provided by the Copyright Office and are reproduced here with Form VA.

The Copyright Office also makes available a free Copyright Information Kit. This includes copies of Form VA and other Copyright Office circulars and is worth requesting. To expedite receiving forms or circulars, the Forms and Circulars Hotline number can be used: (202) 707-9100.

Because of budget constraints, the Copyright Office will accept reproductions of Form VA such as the tear-out form in this book. If the illustrator wishes to make copies, however, the copies must be clear, legible, on a good grade of white paper, and printed on a single sheet of paper so that when the sheet is turned over the top of page 2 is directly behind the top of page 1. Also, the Register of Copyrights has requested an increase in the fees paid to the Copyright Office, so the fee structure should be checked from time to time.

It is wise to register any work that the illustrator feels may be infringed. Registration has a number of values, the most important of which is to establish proof that a particular artwork was created by the artist as of a certain date. Both published and unpublished artworks can be registered. In fact, unpublished artworks can be registered in groups for a single application fee.

For published artworks, the proper deposit is usually two complete copies of the work. For unpublished artworks, one complete copy would be correct. Since the purpose of registering is to protect what the illustrator has created, it is important that the material deposited fully show what is copyrightable.

Obviously, unique artworks cannot be sent along with the application for purposes of identifying themselves, so the Copyright Office accepts other identifying materials. These are usually photographs, photostats, slides, drawings, or other two-dimensional representations of the work. The illustrator should provide as much identifying material as is necessary to show the copyrightable content of the artwork, including any copyright notice which has been used. The proper form for presenting notice of copyright is © or Copyright or Copr., followed by the illustrator's name, and the year of first publication. Since there is some disagreement about whether one-of-a-kind works can ever be published, according to the definition of that term in the copyright law, the year of creation can also be placed on such works.

The preferable size for identifying materials (other than transparencies) is 8 x 10 inches, but anything from 3 x 3 inches to 9 x 12 inches will be acceptable. Also, at least one piece of the identifying material must give an exact measurement of one or more dimensions of the artwork and give the title on its front, back, or mount.

For a full review of registration and its requirements, the illustrator can consult Copyright Office Circular 40, *Copyright Registration for Works of the Visual Arts,* and Circular 40a, *Deposit Requirements of Claims to Copyright in Visual Arts Material.*

A copyright registration is effective as of the date that the Copyright Office receives the application, fee, and deposit materials in an acceptable form, regardless of how long it takes to send back the certificate of registration. It may take 120 days before the certificate of registration is sent to the illustrator. To ensure that the Copyright Office receives the materials, the artist should send them by registered or certified mail with a return receipt requested from the post office.

An illustrator can request information as to the status of an application. However, a fee will be charged by the Copyright Office if such a status report must be given within 120 days of the submission of the application.

For a more extensive discussion of the legal aspects of copyright, the illustrator can consult *Legal Guide for the Visual Artist.*

# Filling Out Application Form VA

*Detach and read these instructions before completing this form. Make sure all applicable spaces have been filled in before you return this form.*

## BASIC INFORMATION

**When to Use This Form:** Use Form VA for copyright registration of published or unpublished works of the visual arts. This category consists of "pictorial, graphic, or sculptural works," including two-dimensional and three-dimensional works of fine, graphic, and applied art, photographs, prints and art reproductions, maps, globes, charts, technical drawings, diagrams, and models.

**What Does Copyright Protect?** Copyright in a work of the visual arts protects those pictorial, graphic, or sculptural elements that, either alone or in combination, represent an "original work of authorship." The statute declares: "In no case does copyright protection for an original work of authorship extend to any idea, procedure, process, system, method of operation, concept, principle, or discovery, regardless of the form in which it is described, explained, illustrated, or embodied in such work."

**Works of Artistic Craftsmanship and Designs:** "Works of artistic craftsmanship" are registrable on Form VA, but the statute makes clear that protection extends to "their form" and not to "their mechanical or utilitarian aspects." The "design of a useful article" is considered copyrightable "only if, and only to the extent that, such design incorporates pictorial, graphic, or sculptural features that can be identified separately from, and are capable of existing independently of, the utilitarian aspects of the article."

**Labels and Advertisements:** Works prepared for use in connection with the sale or advertisement of goods and services are registrable if they contain "original work of authorship." Use Form VA if the copyrightable material in the work you are registering is mainly pictorial or graphic; use Form TX if it consists mainly of text. **NOTE:** Words and short phrases such as names, titles, and slogans cannot be protected by copyright, and the same is true of standard symbols, emblems, and other commonly used graphic designs that are in the public domain. When used commercially, material of that sort can sometimes be protected under state laws of unfair competition or under the Federal trademark laws. For information about trademark registration, write to the Commissioner of Patents and Trademarks, Washington, D.C. 20231.

**Deposit to Accompany Application:** An application for copyright registration must be accompanied by a deposit consisting of copies representing the entire work for which registration is to be made.

**Unpublished Work:** Deposit one complete copy.

**Published Work:** Deposit two complete copies of the best edition.

**Work First Published Outside the United States:** Deposit one complete copy of the first foreign edition.

**Contribution to a Collective Work:** Deposit one complete copy of the best edition of the collective work.

**The Copyright Notice:** For published works, the law provides that a copyright notice in a specified form "shall be placed on all publicly distributed copies from which the work can be visually perceived." Use of the copyright notice is the responsibility of the copyright owner and does not require advance permission from the Copyright Office. The required form of the notice for copies generally consists of three elements: (1) the symbol "©", or the word "Copyright," or the abbreviation "Copr."; (2) the year of first publication; and (3) the name of the owner of copyright. For example: "© 1981 Constance Porter." The notice is to be affixed to the copies "in such manner and location as to give reasonable notice of the claim of copyright."

For further information about copyright registration, notice, or special questions relating to copyright problems, write:

Information and Publications Section, LM-455
Copyright Office, Library of Congress, Washington, D.C. 20559

## LINE-BY-LINE INSTRUCTIONS

## 1 SPACE 1: Title

**Title of This Work:** Every work submitted for copyright registration must be given a title to identify that particular work. If the copies of the work bear a title (or an identifying phrase that could serve as a title), transcribe that wording *completely* and *exactly* on the application. Indexing of the registration and future identification of the work will depend on the information you give here.

**Previous or Alternative Titles:** Complete this space if there are any additional titles for the work under which someone searching for the registration might be likely to look, or under which a document pertaining to the work might be recorded.

**Publication as a Contribution:** If the work being registered is a contribution to a periodical, serial, or collection, give the title of the contribution in the "Title of This Work" space. Then, in the line headed "Publication as a Contribution," give information about the collective work in which the contribution appeared.

**Nature of This Work:** Briefly describe the general nature or character of the pictorial, graphic, or sculptural work being registered for copyright. Examples: "Oil Painting"; "Charcoal Drawing"; "Etching"; "Sculpture"; "Map"; "Photograph"; "Scale Model"; "Lithographic Print"; "Jewelry Design"; "Fabric Design."

## 2 SPACE 2: Author(s)

**General Instructions:** After reading these instructions, decide who are the "authors" of this work for copyright purposes. Then, unless the work is a "collective work," give the requested information about every "author" who contributed any appreciable amount of copyrightable matter to this version of the work. If you need further space, request additional Continuation Sheets. In the case of a collective work, such as a catalog of paintings or collection of cartoons by various authors, give information about the author of the collective work as a whole.

**Name of Author:** The fullest form of the author's name should be given. Unless the work was "made for hire," the individual who actually created the work is its "author." In the case of a work made for hire, the statute provides that "the employer or other person for whom the work was prepared is considered the author."

**What is a "Work Made for Hire"?** A "work made for hire" is defined as: (1) "a work prepared by an employee within the scope of his or her employment"; or (2) "a work specially ordered or commissioned for use as a contribution to a collective work, as a part of a motion picture or other audiovisual work, as a translation, as a supplementary work, as a compilation, as an instructional text, as a test, as answer material for a test, or as an atlas, if the parties expressly agree in a written instrument signed by them that the work shall be considered a work made for hire." If you have checked "Yes" to indicate that the work was "made for hire," you must give the full legal name of the employer (or other person for whom the work was prepared). You may also include the name of the employee along with the name of the employer (for example: "Elster Publishing Co., employer for hire of John Ferguson").

**"Anonymous" or "Pseudonymous" Work:** An author's contribution to a work is "anonymous" if that author is not identified on the copies or phonorecords of the work. An author's contribution to a work is "pseudonymous" if that author is identified on the copies or phonorecords under a fictitious name. If the work is "anonymous" you may: (1) leave the line blank; or (2) state "anonymous" on the line; or (3) reveal the author's identity. If the work is "pseudonymous" you may: (1) leave the line blank; or (2) give the pseudonym and identify it as such (for example: "Huntley Haverstock, pseudonym"); or (3) reveal the author's name, making clear which is the real name and which is the pseudonym (for example: "Henry Leek, whose pseudonym is Priam Farrel"). However, the citizenship or domicile of the author **must** be given in all cases.

**Dates of Birth and Death:** If the author is dead, the statute requires that the year of death be included in the application unless the work is anonymous or pseudonymous. The author's birth date is optional, but is useful as a form of identification. Leave this space blank if the author's contribution was a "work made for hire."

**Author's Nationality or Domicile:** Give the country of which the author is a citizen, or the country in which the author is domiciled. Nationality or domicile **must** be given in all cases.

**Nature of Authorship:** Give a brief general statement of the nature of this particular author's contribution to the work. Examples: "Painting"; "Photograph"; "Silk Screen Reproduction"; "Co-author of Cartographic Material"; "Technical Drawing"; "Text and Artwork."

# 3 SPACE 3: Creation and Publication

**General Instructions:** Do not confuse "creation" with "publication." Every application for copyright registration must state "the year in which creation of the work was completed." Give the date and nation of first publication only if the work has been published.

**Creation:** Under the statute, a work is "created" when it is fixed in a copy or phonorecord for the first time. Where a work has been prepared over a period of time, the part of the work existing in fixed form on a particular date constitutes the created work on that date. The date you give here should be the year in which the author completed the particular version for which registration is now being sought, even if other versions exist or if further changes or additions are planned.

**Publication:** The statute defines "publication" as "the distribution of copies or phonorecords of a work to the public by sale or other transfer of ownership, or by rental, lease, or lending"; a work is also "published" if there has been an "offering to distribute copies or phonorecords to a group of persons for purposes of further distribution, public performance, or public display." Give the full date (month, day, year) when, and the country where, publication first occurred. If first publication took place simultaneously in the United States and other countries, it is sufficient to state "U.S.A."

# 4 SPACE 4: Claimant(s)

**Name(s) and Address(es) of Copyright Claimant(s):** Give the name(s) and address(es) of the copyright claimant(s) in this work even if the claimant is the same as the author. Copyright in a work belongs initially to the author of the work (including, in the case of a work made for hire, the employer or other person for whom the work was prepared). The copyright claimant is either the author of the work or a person or organization to whom the copyright initially belonging to the author has been transferred.

**Transfer:** The statute provides that, if the copyright claimant is not the author, the application for registration must contain "a brief statement of how the claimant obtained ownership of the copyright." If any copyright claimant named in space 4 is not an author named in space 2, give a brief, general statement summarizing the means by which that claimant obtained ownership of the copyright. Examples: "By written contract"; "Transfer of all rights by author"; "Assignment"; "By will." Do not attach transfer documents or other attachments or riders.

# 5 SPACE 5: Previous Registration

**General Instructions:** The questions in space 5 are intended to find out whether an earlier registration has been made for this work and, if so, whether there is any basis for a new registration. As a rule, only one basic copyright registration can be made for the same version of a particular work.

**Same Version:** If this version is substantially the same as the work covered by a previous registration, a second registration is not generally possible unless: (1) the work has been registered in unpublished form and a second registration is now being sought to cover this first published edition; or (2) some-

one other than the author is identified as copyright claimant in the earlier registration, and the author is now seeking registration in his or her own name. If either of these two exceptions apply, check the appropriate box and give the earlier registration number and date. Otherwise, do not submit Form VA; instead, write the Copyright Office for information about supplementary registration or recordation of transfers of copyright ownership.

**Changed Version:** If the work has been changed, and you are now seeking registration to cover the additions or revisions, check the last box in space 5, give the earlier registration number and date, and complete both parts of space 6 in accordance with the instructions below.

**Previous Registration Number and Date:** If more than one previous registration has been made for the work, give the number and date of the latest registration.

# 6 SPACE 6: Derivative Work or Compilation

**General Instructions:** Complete space 6 if this work is a "changed version," "compilation," or "derivative work," and if it incorporates one or more earlier works that have already been published or registered for copyright, or that have fallen into the public domain. A "compilation" is defined as "a work formed by the collection and assembling of preexisting materials or of data that are selected, coordinated, or arranged in such a way that the resulting work as a whole constitutes an original work of authorship." A "derivative work" is "a work based on one or more preexisting works." Examples of derivative works include reproductions of works of art, sculptures based on drawings, lithographs based on paintings, maps based on previously published sources, or "any other form in which a work may be recast, transformed, or adapted." Derivative works also include works "consisting of editorial revisions, annotations, or other modifications" if these changes, as a whole, represent an original work of authorship.

**Preexisting Material (space 6a):** Complete this space **and** space 6b for derivative works. In this space identify the preexisting work that has been recast, transformed, or adapted. Examples of preexisting material might be "Grunewald Altarpiece"; or "19th century quilt design." Do not complete this space for compilations.

**Material Added to This Work (space 6b):** Give a brief, general statement of the **additional** new material covered by the copyright claim for which registration is sought. In the case of a derivative work, identify this new material. Examples: "Adaptation of design and additional artistic work"; "Reproduction of painting by photolithography"; "Additional cartographic material"; "Compilation of photographs." If the work is a compilation, give a brief, general statement describing both the material that has been compiled **and** the compilation itself. Example: "Compilation of 19th Century Political Cartoons."

# 7,8,9 SPACE 7, 8, 9: Fee, Correspondence, Certification, Return Address

**Deposit Account:** If you maintain a Deposit Account in the Copyright Office, identify it in space 7. Otherwise leave the space blank and send the fee of $10 with your application and deposit.

**Correspondence (space 7):** This space should contain the name, address, area code, and telephone number of the person to be consulted if correspondence about this application becomes necessary.

**Certification (space 8):** The application cannot be accepted unless it bears the date and the **handwritten signature** of the author or other copyright claimant, or of the owner of exclusive right(s), or of the duly authorized agent of the author, claimant, or owner of exclusive right(s).

**Address for Return of Certificate (space 9):** The address box must be completed legibly since the certificate will be returned in a window envelope.

# MORE INFORMATION

## Form of Deposit for Works of the Visual Arts

**Exceptions to General Deposit Requirements:** As explained on the reverse side of this page, the statutory deposit requirements (generally one copy for unpublished works and two copies for published works) will vary for particular kinds of works of the visual arts. The copyright law authorizes the Register of Copyrights to issue regulations specifying "the administrative classes into which works are to be placed for purposes of deposit and registration, and the nature of the copies or phonorecords to be deposited in the various classes specified." For particular classes, the regulations may require or permit "the deposit of identifying material instead of copies or phonorecords," or "the deposit of only one copy or phonorecord where two would normally be required."

## What Should You Deposit? The detailed requirements with respect to the
kind of deposit to accompany an application on Form VA are contained in the Copyright

Office Regulations. The following does not cover all of the deposit requirements, but is intended to give you some general guidance.

**For an Unpublished Work,** the material deposited should represent the entire copyrightable content of the work for which registration is being sought.

**For a Published Work,** the material deposited should generally consist of two complete copies of the best edition. Exceptions: (1) For certain types of works, one complete copy may be deposited instead of two. These include greeting cards, postcards, stationery, labels, advertisements, scientific drawings, and globes; (2) For most three-dimensional sculptural works, and for certain two-dimensional works, the Copyright Office Regulations require deposit of identifying material (photographs or drawings in a specified form) rather than copies; and (3) Under certain circumstances, for works published in five copies or less or in limited, numbered editions, the deposit may consist of one copy or of identifying reproductions.

# FORM VA
UNITED STATES COPYRIGHT OFFICE

REGISTRATION NUMBER

_____
VA                          VAU

EFFECTIVE DATE OF REGISTRATION

_____

| Month | Day | Year |

**DO NOT WRITE ABOVE THIS LINE. IF YOU NEED MORE SPACE, USE A SEPARATE CONTINUATION SHEET.**

## 1

**TITLE OF THIS WORK ▼**

**NATURE OF THIS WORK ▼** See instructions

**PREVIOUS OR ALTERNATIVE TITLES ▼**

**PUBLICATION AS A CONTRIBUTION** If this work was published as a contribution to a periodical, serial, or collection, give information about the collective work in which the contribution appeared. **Title of Collective Work ▼**

If published in a periodical or serial give: **Volume ▼**     **Number ▼**     **Issue Date ▼**     **On Pages ▼**

## 2

**a**

**NAME OF AUTHOR ▼**

**DATES OF BIRTH AND DEATH**
Year Born ▼     Year Died ▼

Was this contribution to the work a "work made for hire"?
☐ Yes
☐ No

**AUTHOR'S NATIONALITY OR DOMICILE**
Name of Country
OR { Citizen of ▶_____
{ Domiciled in ▶_____

**WAS THIS AUTHOR'S CONTRIBUTION TO THE WORK**
Anonymous? ☐ Yes ☐ No
Pseudonymous? ☐ Yes ☐ No
If the answer to either of these questions is "Yes," see detailed instructions.

**NATURE OF AUTHORSHIP** Briefly describe nature of the material created by this author in which copyright is claimed. ▼

### NOTE
Under the law, the "author" of a "work made for hire" is generally the employer, not the employee (see instructions). For any part of this work that was "made for hire" check "Yes" in the space provided, give the employer (or other person for whom the work was prepared) as "Author" of that part, and leave the space for dates of birth and death blank.

**b**

**NAME OF AUTHOR ▼**

**DATES OF BIRTH AND DEATH**
Year Born ▼     Year Died ▼

Was this contribution to the work a "work made for hire"?
☐ Yes
☐ No

**AUTHOR'S NATIONALITY OR DOMICILE**
Name of country
OR { Citizen of ▶_____
{ Domiciled in ▶_____

**WAS THIS AUTHOR'S CONTRIBUTION TO THE WORK**
Anonymous? ☐ Yes ☐ No
Pseudonymous? ☐ Yes ☐ No
If the answer to either of these questions is "Yes," see detailed instructions.

**NATURE OF AUTHORSHIP** Briefly describe nature of the material created by this author in which copyright is claimed. ▼

**c**

**NAME OF AUTHOR ▼**

**DATES OF BIRTH AND DEATH**
Year Born ▼     Year Died ▼

Was this contribution to the work a "work made for hire"?
☐ Yes
☐ No

**AUTHOR'S NATIONALITY OR DOMICILE**
Name of Country
OR { Citizen of ▶_____
{ Domiciled in ▶_____

**WAS THIS AUTHOR'S CONTRIBUTION TO THE WORK**
Anonymous? ☐ Yes ☐ No
Pseudonymous? ☐ Yes ☐ No
If the answer to either of these questions is "Yes," see detailed instructions.

**NATURE OF AUTHORSHIP** Briefly describe nature of the material created by this author in which copyright is claimed. ▼

## 3

**YEAR IN WHICH CREATION OF THIS WORK WAS COMPLETED** This information must be given in all cases. ◀ Year

**DATE AND NATION OF FIRST PUBLICATION OF THIS PARTICULAR WORK**
Complete this information ONLY if this work has been published. Month ▶_____ Day ▶_____ Year ▶_____ ◀ Nation

## 4

See instructions before completing this space.

**COPYRIGHT CLAIMANT(S)** Name and address must be given even if the claimant is the same as the author given in space 2.▼

**TRANSFER** If the claimant(s) named here in space 4 are different from the author(s) named in space 2, give a brief statement of how the claimant(s) obtained ownership of the copyright.▼

**DO NOT WRITE HERE OFFICE USE ONLY**

APPLICATION RECEIVED
_____
ONE DEPOSIT RECEIVED
_____
TWO DEPOSITS RECEIVED
_____
REMITTANCE NUMBER AND DATE

**MORE ON BACK ▶** • Complete all applicable spaces (numbers 5-9) on the reverse side of this page.
• See detailed instructions.     • Sign the form at line 8.

**DO NOT WRITE HERE**

Page 1 of _____ pages

| EXAMINED BY | **FORM VA** |
|---|---|
| CHECKED BY | |

☐ CORRESPONDENCE Yes

☐ DEPOSIT ACCOUNT FUNDS USED

FOR COPYRIGHT OFFICE USE ONLY

**DO NOT WRITE ABOVE THIS LINE. IF YOU NEED MORE SPACE, USE A SEPARATE CONTINUATION SHEET.**

**PREVIOUS REGISTRATION** Has registration for this work, or for an earlier version of this work, already been made in the Copyright Office?
☐ **Yes** ☐ **No** If your answer is "Yes," why is another registration being sought? (Check appropriate box) ▼

☐ This is the first published edition of a work previously registered in unpublished form.

☐ This is the first application submitted by this author as copyright claimant.

☐ This is a changed version of the work, as shown by space 6 on this application.

If your answer is "Yes," give: **Previous Registration Number** ▼      **Year of Registration** ▼

**5**

**DERIVATIVE WORK OR COMPILATION** Complete both space 6a & 6b for a derivative work; complete only 6b for a compilation.
**a. Preexisting Material** Identify any preexisting work or works that this work is based on or incorporates. ▼

**b. Material Added to This Work** Give a brief, general statement of the material that has been added to this work and in which copyright is claimed. ▼

**6**

See instructions before completing this space.

**DEPOSIT ACCOUNT** If the registration fee is to be charged to a Deposit Account established in the Copyright Office, give name and number of Account.
**Name** ▼      **Account Number** ▼

**7**

**CORRESPONDENCE** Give name and address to which correspondence about this application should be sent. Name/Address/Apt/City/State/Zip ▼

Area Code & Telephone Number ▶

Be sure to give your daytime phone number. ◀

**CERTIFICATION*** I, the undersigned, hereby certify that I am the
Check only one ▼

☐ author
☐ other copyright claimant
☐ owner of exclusive right(s)
☐ authorized agent of _____
Name of author or other copyright claimant, or owner of exclusive right(s) ▲

**8**

of the work identified in this application and that the statements made
by me in this application are correct to the best of my knowledge.

**Typed or printed name and date** ▼ If this is a published work, this date must be the same as or later than the date of publication given in space 3.

_____ date ▶ _____

Handwritten signature (X) ▼

**MAIL CERTIFI-CATE TO**

**Certificate will be mailed in window envelope**

Name ▼

Number/Street/Apartment Number ▼

City/State/ZIP ▼

**Have you:**
● Completed all necessary spaces?
● Signed your application in space 8?
● Enclosed check or money order for $10 payable to *Register of Copyrights*?
● Enclosed your deposit material with the application and fee?

**MAIL TO:** Register of Copyrights. Library of Congress, Washington. D.C. 20559

**9**

U.S. GOVERNMENT PRINTING OFFICE: 1988 202-133 80.008

August 1988- 60.000

# THE FORMS

## TEAR-OUT SECTION

**Forms Available on Computer Disk**

For ease of modification, the forms may be purchased on computer disk in the following formats: WordPerfect 4.2 and PageMaker for the IBM and compatibles, Microsoft Word 3.1 and PageMaker for the Macintosh. For further information, please write Allworth Press, 10 East 23rd Street, New York, NY 10010

# Estimate

Client _____ Date _____

Address _____

Client Purchase Order Number _____ Job Number _____

This Estimate is based on the specifications and terms which follow. If the Client confirms that the Illustrator should proceed with the assignment based on this Estimate, it is understood that the assignment shall be subject to the terms shown on this Estimate and that Client shall sign a Confirmation of Assignment form incorporating the same specifications and terms. If the assignment proceeds without a Confirmation of Assignment being signed by both parties, the assignment shall be governed by the terms and conditions contained in this Estimate.

1. **Description.** The Illustrator shall create the Work in accordance with the following specifications:
   Subject matter _____
   Number of illustrations in color _____
   Number of illustrations in black and white _____
   Size of illustrations _____
   Medium for illustrations _____
   Other specifications _____

2. **Due Date.** Sketches shall be delivered within _____ days after either the Client's authorization to commence work or, if the Client is to provide reference, layouts, or specifications, after the Client has provided same to the Illustrator, whichever occurs later. Finished art shall be delivered _____ days after the approval of sketches by the Client.

3. **Grant of Rights.** Upon receipt of full payment, the Illustrator shall grant to the Client the following rights in the finished art:
   For use as _____
   For the product or publication named _____
   In the following territory _____
   For the following time period _____
   Other limitations _____
   With respect to the usage shown above, the Client shall have ❑ exclusive ❑ nonexclusive rights.
   If the finished art is for use as a contribution to a magazine, the grant of rights shall be first North American serial rights only unless specified to the contrary above.

4. **Reservation of Rights.** All rights not expressly granted shall be reserved to the Illustrator, including but not limited to all rights in sketches, comps, or other preliminary materials.

5. **Fee.** Client shall pay the following purchase price: $_____ for the usage rights granted. Client shall also pay sales tax, if required.

6. **Additional Usage.** If Client wishes to make any additional uses of the Work, Client shall seek permission from the Illustrator and pay an additional fee to be agreed upon.

7. **Expenses.** Client shall reimburse the Illustrator for the following expenses: ❑ Messenger ❑ Models ❑ Props ❑ Travel ❑ Telephone ❑ Other _____ At the time of signing the Confirmation of Assignment or the commencement of work, whichever is first, Client shall pay Illustrator $_____ as a nonrefundable advance against expenses. If the advance exceeds expenses incurred, the credit balance shall be used to reduce the fee payable, or, if the fee has been fully paid, shall be reimbursed to Client.

8. **Payment.** Client shall pay the Illustrator within thirty days of the date of Illustrator's billing, which shall be dated as of the date of delivery of the finished art. In the event that work is postponed at the request of the Client, the Illustrator shall have the right to bill pro rata for work completed through the date of that request, while reserving all other rights. Overdue payments shall be subject to interest charges of _____ percent monthly.

9. **Advances.** At the time of signing the Confirmation of Assignment or the commencement of work, whichever is first, Client shall pay Illustrator _____ percent of the fee as an advance against the total fee. Upon approval of sketches Client shall pay Illustrator _____ percent of the fee as an advance against the total fee.

10. **Revisions.** The Illustrator shall be given the first opportunity to make any revisions requested by the Client. If the revisions are not due to any fault on the part of the Illustrator, an additional fee shall be charged. If the Illustrator objects to any revisions to be made by the Client, the Illustrator shall have the right to have his or her name removed from the published Work.

11. **Copyright Notice.** Copyright notice in the name of the Illustrator ❑ shall ❑ shall not accompany the Work when it is reproduced.

12. **Authorship Credit.** Authorship credit in the name of the Illustrator ❑ shall ❑ shall not accompany the Work when it is reproduced. If the finished art is used as a contribution to a magazine or for a book, authorship credit shall be given unless specified to the contrary in the preceding sentence.

13. **Cancellation.** In the event of cancellation by the Client, the following cancellation payment shall be paid by the Client: **(A)** Cancellation prior to the finished art being turned in: _____ percent of fee; **(B)** Cancellation due to finished art being unsatisfactory: _____ percent of fee; and **(C)** Cancellation for any other reason after the finished art is turned in: _____ percent of fee. In the event of cancellation, the Client shall also pay any expenses incurred by the Illustrator and the Illustrator shall own all rights in the Work. The billing upon cancellation shall be payable within thirty days of the Client's notification to stop work or the delivery of the finished art, whichever occurs sooner.

14. **Ownership and Return of Artwork.** The ownership of original artwork, including sketches and any other materials created in the process of making the finished art, shall remain with the Illustrator. All such artwork shall be returned to the Illustrator by bonded messenger, air freight, or registered mail within thirty days of the Client's completing its use of the artwork. Based on the specifications for the Work, a reasonable value for the original, finished art is $_____.

15. **Permissions and Releases.** The Client shall indemnify and hold harmless the Illustrator against any and all claims, costs, and expenses, including attorney's fees, due to materials included in the work at the request of the Client for which no copyright permission or privacy release was requested or uses which exceed the uses allowed pursuant to a permission or release.

16. **Arbitration.** All disputes shall be submitted to binding arbitration before _____ in the following location _____ and settled in accordance with the rules of the American Arbitration Association. Judgment upon the arbitration award may be entered in any court having jurisdiction thereof. Disputes in which the amount at issue is less than $_____ shall not be subject to this arbitration provision.

17. **Miscellany.** If the Client authorizes the Illustrator to commence work, the terms of this Estimate Form shall be binding upon the parties, their heirs, successors, assigns, and personal representatives; the Estimate Form constitutes the entire understanding between the parties; its terms can be modified only by an instrument in writing signed by both parties, except that the Client may authorize expenses and revisions orally; a waiver of a breach of any of its provisions shall not be construed as a continuing waiver of other breaches of the same or other provisions hereof; and the relationship between the Client and Illustrator shall be governed by the laws of the State of _____.

Illustrator _____

# Confirmation of Assignment

AGREEMENT as of the _____ day of _____, 19 _____, between _____,
(hereinafter referred to as the "Client"), located at _____,
and _____ (hereinafter referred to as the "Illustrator"),
located at _____, with
respect to the creation of certain illustrations (hereinafter referred to as the "Work").

WHEREAS, Illustrator is a professional illustrator of good standing;

WHEREAS, Client wishes the Illustrator to create certain Work described more fully herein; and

WHEREAS, Illustrator wishes to create such Work;

NOW, THEREFORE, in consideration of the foregoing premises and the mutual covenants hereinafter set forth and other valuable considerations, the parties hereto agree as follows:

1. **Description.** The Illustrator agrees to create the Work in accordance with the following specifications:

   Subject matter _____

   Number of illustrations in color _____

   Number of illustrations in black and white _____

   Size of illustrations _____

   Medium for illustrations _____

   Other specifications _____

   Client purchase order number _____ Job number _____

2. **Due Date.** The Illustrator agrees to deliver sketches within _____ days after the later of the signing of this Agreement or, if the Client is to provide reference, layouts, or specifications, after the Client has provided same to the Illustrator. Finished art shall be delivered _____ days after the approval of sketches by the Client.

3. **Grant of Rights.** Upon receipt of full payment, the Illustrator grants to the Client the following rights in the finished art:

   For use as _____

   For the product or publication named _____

   In the following territory _____

   For the following time period _____

   Other limitations _____

   With respect to the usage shown above, the Client shall have ❑ exclusive ❑ nonexclusive rights.

   If the finished art is for use as a contribution to a magazine, the grant of rights shall be for first North American serial rights only unless specified to the contrary above.

4. **Reservation of Rights.** All rights not expressly granted hereunder are reserved to the Illustrator, including but not limited to all rights in sketches, comps, or other preliminary materials.

5. **Fee.** Client agrees to pay the following purchase price: $_____ for the usage rights granted. Client agrees to pay sales tax, if required.

6. **Additional Usage.** If Client wishes to make any additional uses of the Work, Client agrees to seek permission from the Illustrator and make such payments as are agreed to between the parties at that time.

7. **Expenses.** Client agrees to reimburse the Illustrator for the following expenses: ❑ Messengers ❑ Models ❑ Props ❑ Travel ❑ Telephone ❑ Other _____

   At the time of signing this Agreement, Client shall pay Illustrator $_____ as a nonrefundable advance against expenses. If the advance exceeds expenses incurred, the credit balance shall be used to reduce the fee payable or, if the fee has been fully paid, shall be reimbursed to Client.

8. **Payment.** Client agrees to pay the Illustrator within thirty days of the date of Illustrator's billing, which shall be dated as of the date of delivery of the finished art. In the event that work is postponed at the request of the Client, the Illustrator shall have the right to bill pro rata for work completed through the date of that request, while reserving all other rights under this Agreement. Overdue payments shall be subject to interest charges of _____ percent monthly.

9. **Advances.** At the time of signing this Agreement, Client shall pay Illustrator ____ percent of the fee as an advance against the total fee. Upon approval of sketches Client shall pay Illustrator ____ percent of the fee as an advance against the total fee.

10. **Revisions.** The Illustrator shall be given the first opportunity to make any revisions requested by the Client. If the revisions are not due to any fault on the part of the Illustrator, an additional fee shall be charged. If the Illustrator objects to any revisions to be made by the Client, the Illustrator shall have the right to have his or her name removed from the published Work.

11. **Copyright Notice.** Copyright notice in the Illustrator's name ❏ shall ❏ shall not be published with the Work.

12. **Authorship Credit.** Authorship credit in the name of the Illustrator ❏ shall ❏ shall not accompany the Work when it is reproduced. If the finished art is used as a contribution to a magazine or for a book, authorship credit shall be given unless specified to the contrary in the preceding sentence.

13. **Cancellation.** In the event of cancellation by the Client, the following cancellation payment shall be paid by the Client: **(A)** Cancellation prior to the finished art being turned in: ____% of fee; **(B)** Cancellation due to finished art being unsatisfactory: ____% of fee; and **(C)** Cancellation for any other reason after the finished art is turned in: ____% of fee. In the event of cancellation, the Client shall also pay any expenses incurred by the Illustrator and the Illustrator shall own all rights in the Work. The billing upon cancellation shall be payable within thirty days of the Client's notification to stop work or the delivery of the finished art, whichever occurs sooner.

14. **Ownership and Return of Artwork.** The ownership of original artwork, including sketches and any other materials created in the process of making the finished art, shall remain with the Illustrator. All such artwork shall be returned to the Illustrator by bonded messenger, air freight, or registered mail within thirty days of the Client's completing its use of the artwork. The parties agree that the value of the original, finished art is $_____.

15. **Permissions and Releases.** The Client agrees to indemnify and hold harmless the Illustrator against any and all claims, costs, and expenses, including attorney's fees, due to materials included in the Work at the request of the Client for which no copyright permission or privacy release was requested or uses which exceed the uses allowed pursuant to a permission or release.

16. **Arbitration.** All disputes arising under this Agreement shall be submitted to binding arbitration before _____ in the following location _____ and settled in accordance with the rules of the American Arbitration Association. Judgment upon the arbitration award may be entered in any court having jurisdiction thereof. Disputes in which the amount at issue is less than $_____ shall not be subject to this arbitration provision.

17. **Miscellany.** This Agreement shall be binding upon the parties hereto, their heirs, successors, assigns, and personal representatives. This Agreement constitutes the entire understanding between the parties. Its terms can be modified only by an instrument in writing signed by both parties, except that the Client may authorize expenses or revisions orally. A waiver of a breach of any of the provisions of this Agreement shall not be construed as a continuing waiver of other breaches of the same or other provisions hereof. This Agreement shall be governed by the laws of the State of _____.

IN WITNESS WHEREOF, the parties hereto have signed this Agreement as of the date first set forth above.

Illustrator _____

Client _____
Company Name

By _____
Authorized Signatory, Title

# Illustrator—Agent Contract

AGREEMENT, entered into as of this _____ day of _____, 19_____, between _____ (hereinafter referred to as the "Illustrator"), located at _____, and _____ (hereinafter referred to as the "Agent"), located at _____.

WHEREAS, the Illustrator is an established illustrator of proven talents; and

WHEREAS, the Illustrator wishes to have an agent represent him or her in marketing certain rights enumerated herein; and

WHEREAS, the Agent is capable of marketing the artwork produced by the Illustrator; and

WHEREAS, the Agent wishes to represent the Illustrator;

NOW, THEREFORE, in consideration of the foregoing premises and the mutual covenants hereinafter set forth and other valuable consideration, the parties hereto agree as follows:

1. **Agency**. The Illustrator appoints the Agent to act as his or her representative:

    **(A)** in the following geographical area _____

    **(B)** for the following markets:

    - ❏ Advertising
    - ❏ Corporate
    - ❏ Book publishing
    - ❏ Magazines
    - ❏ Other, specified as _____

    **(C)** to be the Illustrator's ❏ exclusive ❏ nonexclusive agent in the area and markets indicated.

    Any rights not granted to the Agent are reserved to the Illustrator.

2. **Best Efforts.** The Agent agrees to use his or her best efforts in submitting the Illustrator's work for the purpose of securing assignments for the Illustrator. The Agent shall negotiate the terms of any assignment that is offered, but the Illustrator may reject any assignment if he or she finds the terms thereof unacceptable.

3. **Samples.** The Illustrator shall provide the Agent with such samples of work as are from time to time necessary for the purpose of securing assignments. These samples shall remain the property of the Illustrator and be returned on termination of this Agreement. The Agent shall take reasonable efforts to protect the work from loss or damage, but shall be liable for such loss or damage only if caused by the Agent's negligence.

4. **Term.** This Agreement shall take effect as of the date first set forth above, and remain in full force and effect for a term of one year, unless terminated as provided in Paragraph 11.

5. **Commissions.** The Agent shall be entitled to the following commissions: **(A)** On assignments obtained by the Agent during the term of this Agreement, _____ percent of the billing. **(B)** On house accounts, _____ percent of the billing. For purposes of this Agreement, house accounts are defined as accounts obtained by the Illustrator at any time or obtained by another agent representing the Illustrator prior to the commencement of this Agreement and are listed in the Schedule of House Accounts attached to this Agreement. **(C)** For books which the Illustrator authors or coauthors, _____ percent of the royalties or licensing proceeds paid to the Illustrator by the publisher or its licensees.

    It is understood by both parties that no commissions shall be paid on assignments rejected by the Illustrator or for which the Illustrator fails to receive payment, regardless of the reason payment is not made. Further, no commissions shall be payable in either **(A)** or **(B)** above for any part of the billing that is due to expenses incurred by the Illustrator in performing the assignment, whether or not such expenses are reimbursed by the client. In the event that a flat fee is paid by the client, it shall be reduced by the amount of expenses incurred by the Illustrator in performing the assignment, and the Agent's commission shall be payable only on the fee as reduced for expenses.

6. **Billing.** The ❏ Illustrator ❏ Agent shall be responsible for all billings.

7. **Payments.** The party responsible for billing shall make all payments due within _____ days of receipt of any fees covered by this Agreement. Such payments due shall be be deemed trust funds and shall not be inter-mingled with funds belonging to the party responsible for billing and payment. Late payments shall be accom-panied by interest calculated at the rate of _____ percent per month thereafter.

8. **Promotional Expenses.** Promotional expenses, including but not limited to promotional mailings and paid advertising, shall be mutually agreed to by the parties and paid _____ percent by the Agent and _____ per-cent by the Illustrator. The Agent shall bear the expenses of shipping, insurance, and similar marketing expenses.

9. **Accountings.** The party responsible for billing shall send copies of invoices to the other party when rendered. If requested, that party shall also provide the other party with semiannual accountings showing all assignments for the period, the clients' names and addresses, the fees paid, expenses incurred by the Illustrator, the dates of payment, the amounts on which the Agent's commissions are to be calculated, and the sums due less those amounts already paid.

10. **Inspection of the Books and Records.** The party responsible for the billing shall keep the books and records with respect to payments due each party at his or her place of business and permit the other party to inspect these books and records during normal business hours on the giving of reasonable notice.

11. **Termination.** This Agreement may be terminated by either party by giving thirty (30) days written notice to the other party. If the Illustrator receives assignments after the termination date from clients originally obtained by the Agent during the term of this Agreement, the commission specified in Paragraph 5(A) shall be payable to the Agent under the following circumstances. If the Agent has represented the Illustrator for _____ months or less, the Agent shall receive a commission on such assignments received by the Illustrator within _____ days of the date of termination. This period shall increase by thirty (30) days for each additional _____ months that the Agent has represented the Illustrator, but in no event shall such period exceed _____ days. In the event of the bankruptcy or insolvency of the Agent, this Agreement shall also terminate. The rights and obligations under Paragraphs 3, 6, 7, 8, 9, and 10 shall survive termination.

12. **Assignment.** This Agreement shall not be assigned by either of the parties hereto. It shall be binding on and inure to the benefit of the successors, admininstrators, executors, or heirs of the Agent and Illustrator.

13. **Arbitration.** Any disputes arising under this Agreement shall be settled by arbitration before _____ under the rules of the American Arbitration Association in the City of _____, except that the par-ties shall have the right to go to court for claims of $_____ or less. Any award rendered by the arbitrator may be entered in any court having jurisdiction thereof.

14. **Notices.** All notices shall be given to the parties at their respective addresses set forth above.

15. **Independent Contractor Status.** Both parties agree that the Agent is acting as an independent contractor. This Agreement is not an employment agreement, nor does it constitute a joint venture or partnership between the Illustrator and Agent.

16. **Amendments and Merger.** All amendments to this Agreement must be written. This Agreement incorporates the entire understanding of the parties.

17. **Governing Law.** This Agreement shall be governed by the laws of the State of _____ .

IN WITNESS WHEREOF, the parties have signed this Agreement as of the date set forth above.

Illustrator_____     Agent_____

**Schedule of House Accounts**

Date_____

1._____
(name and address of client)

2._____

3._____

4._____

5._____

6._____

7._____

8._____

9._____

10._____

11._____

12._____

13._____

14._____

15._____

16._____

17._____

18._____

19._____

20._____

# Book Publishing Contract

AGREEMENT, entered into as of this _____ day of _____, 19___, between _____ (hereinafter referred to as the "Publisher"), located at _____, and _____ (hereinafter referred to as the "Illustrator"), located at _____.

WHEREAS, the Illustrator wishes to create a book on the subject of _____ (hereinafter referred to as the "Work")

WHEREAS, the Publisher is familiar with the work of the Illustrator and wishes to publish a book by the Illustrator; and

WHEREAS, the parties wish to have said publication performed subject to the mutual obligations, covenants, and conditions herein.

NOW, THEREFORE, in consideration of the foregoing premises and the mutual covenants hereinafter set forth and other valuable considerations, the parties hereto agree as follows:

1. **Grant of Rights.** The Illustrator grants, conveys, and transfers to the Publisher in that unpublished Work titled _____, certain limited, exclusive rights as follows: **(A)** To publish the Work in the form of a _____ book; **(B)** In the territory of _____; **(C)** In the_____ language; and **(D)** For a term of _____ years.

2. **Reservation of Rights.** All rights not specifically granted to the Publisher are reserved to the Illustrator.

3. **Delivery of Manuscript.** On or before the _____ day of _____, 19_____, the Illustrator shall deliver to the Publisher a complete manuscript of approximately _____ words, which shall be reasonably satisfactory in form and content to the Publisher and in conformity with any outline or description attached hereto and made part hereof. The manuscript shall include the additional materials listed in Paragraph 4 (except that if an index is to be provided by the Illustrator, it shall be delivered to the Publisher within thirty days of Illustrator's receipt of paginated galleys). If the Illustrator fails to deliver the complete manuscript within ninety days after receiving notice from the Publisher of failure to deliver on time, the Publisher shall have the right to terminate this Agreement and receive back from the Illustrator all monies advanced to the Illustrator pursuant to Paragraphs 4, 5, and 9. If the Illustrator delivers a manuscript which, after being given detailed instructions for revisions by the Publisher and _____ days to complete such revisions, is not reasonably acceptable to the Publisher, then monies advanced to the Illustrator pursuant to Paragraphs 4, 5, and 9 shall be ❑ retained by the Illustrator ❑ repaid to the Publisher ❑ repaid to the Publisher only in the event the Illustrator subsequently signs a contract with another Publisher for the Work.

4. **Additional Materials.** The following materials shall be provided by the Illustrator _____ _____ _____ _____. The cost of providing these additional materials shall be borne by the Illustrator, provided, however, that the Publisher at the time of signing this Agreement shall give a nonrefundable payment of $_____ to assist the Illustrator in defraying these costs, which payment shall not be deemed an advance to the Illustrator and shall not be recouped as such.

5. **Permissions.** The Illustrator agrees to obtain all permissions that are necessary for the use of materials copyrighted by others. The cost of providing these permissions shall be borne by the Illustrator, provided, however, that the Publisher at the time of signing this Agreement shall give a nonrefundable payment of $_____ to assist the Illustrator in defraying these costs, which payment shall not be deemed an advance to the Illustrator and shall not be recouped as such. Permissions shall be obtained in writing and copies shall be provided to the Publisher when the manuscript is delivered.

6. **Duty to Publish.** The Publisher shall publish the Work within _____ months of the delivery of the complete manuscript. Failure to so publish shall give the Illustrator the right to terminate this Agreement ninety days after giving written notice to the Publisher of the failure to make timely publication. In the event of such termination, the Illustrator shall have no obligation to return monies received pursuant to Paragraphs 4, 5, and 9.

7. **Royalties.** The Publisher shall pay the Illustrator the following royalties: ____ percent of the suggested retail price on the first 5,000 copies sold; ____ percent of the suggested retail price on the next 5,000 copies sold; and ____ percent of the suggested retail price on all copies sold thereafter. These royalty rates shall be discounted only in the following circumstances: _____
_____

All copies sold shall be cumulated for purposes of escalations in the royalty rates, including revised editions, except for editions in a different form (such as a paperback reprint of a hardcover original) which shall be cumulated separately. Copies sold shall be reduced by copies returned in the same royalty category in which the copies were originally reported as sold.

In the event the Publisher has the right pursuant to Paragraph 1(A) to publish the Work in more than one form, the royalty rates specified above shall apply to publication in the form of a _____ book and the royalty rates for other forms shall be specified here: _____
_____
_____

8. **Subsidiary Rights.** The following subsidiary rights may be licensed by the party indicated and the proceeds divided as specified herein:

| Subsidiary Right | Right to License | | Division of Proceeds | |
|---|---|---|---|---|
| | Illustrator | Publisher | Illustrator | Publisher |
| _____ | _____ | _____ | _____ | _____ |
| _____ | _____ | _____ | _____ | _____ |
| _____ | _____ | _____ | _____ | _____ |
| _____ | _____ | _____ | _____ | _____ |
| _____ | _____ | _____ | _____ | _____ |

If the division of proceeds for any subsidiary right changes after the sale of a certain number of copies, indicate which right, the number of copies required to be sold, and the new division of proceeds _____
_____
_____

The Publisher shall have no rights pursuant to this Paragraph 8 if Publisher is in default of any of its obligations under this Agreement. The right to license any subsidiary right not set forth in this Paragraph is retained by the Illustrator. Licensing income shall be divided as specified herein without any reductions for expenses.

Licensing income shall be collected by the party authorized to license the right and the appropriate percentage remitted by that party to the other party within ten days of receipt. Copies of all licenses shall be provided to both parties immediately upon receipt.

9. **Advances.** The Publisher shall, at the time of signing this Agreement, pay to the Illustrator a nonrefundable advance of $_____, which advance shall be recouped by the Publisher from payments due to the Illustrator pursuant to Paragraph 11 of this Agreement.

10. **Accountings.** Commencing as of the date of publication, the Publisher shall report every ____ months to the Illustrator, showing for that period and cumulatively to date the number of copies printed and bound, the number of copies sold and returned for each royalty rate, the number of copies distributed free for publicity pur-

poses, the number of copies remaindered, destroyed, or lost, and the royalties paid to and owed to the Illustrator. If the Publisher sets up a reserve against returns of books, the reserve may only be set up for the four accounting periods following the first publication of the Work and shall in no event exceed 15 percent of royalties due to the Illustrator in any period.

11. **Payments.** The Publisher shall pay the Illustrator all monies due Illustrator pursuant to Paragraph 10 within thirty days of the close of each accounting period.

12. **Right of Inspection.** The Illustrator shall, upon the giving of written notice, have the right to inspect the Publisher's books of account to verify the accountings. If errors in any such accounting are found to be to the Illustrator's disadvantage and represent more than 5 percent of the payment to the Illustrator pursuant to the said accounting, the cost of inspection shall be paid by the Publisher.

13. **Copyright and Authorship Credit.** The Publisher shall, as an express condition of receiving the grant of rights specified in Paragraph 1, take the necessary steps to register the copyright on behalf of the Illustrator and in the Illustrator's name and shall place copyright notice in the Illustrator's name on all copies of the Work. The Illustrator shall receive authorship credit as follows: _____.

14. **Warranty and Indemnity.** The Illustrator warrants and represents that he or she is the sole creator of the Work and owns all rights granted under this Agreement, that the Work is an original creation and has not previously been published (indicate any parts that have been previously published), that the Work does not infringe any other person's copyrights or rights of literary property, nor, to his or her knowledge, does it violate the rights of privacy of, or libel, other persons. The Illustrator agrees to indemnify the Publisher against any final judgment for damages (after all appeals have been exhausted) in any lawsuit based on an actual breach of the foregoing warranties. In addition, the Illustrator shall pay the Publisher's reasonable costs and attorney's fees incurred in defending such a lawsuit, unless the Illustrator chooses to retain his or her own attorney to defend such lawsuit. The Illustrator makes no warranties and shall have no obligation to indemnify the Publisher with respect to materials inserted in the Work at the Publisher's request. Notwithstanding any of the foregoing, in no event shall the Illustrator's liability under this Paragraph exceed $_____ or _____ percent of sums payable to the Illustrator under this Agreement, whichever is the lesser. In the event a lawsuit is brought which may result in the Illustrator having breached his or her warranties under this Paragraph, the Publisher shall have the right to withhold and place in an escrow account _____ percent of sums payable to the Illustrator pursuant to Paragraph 11, but in no event may said withholding exceed the damages alleged in the complaint.

15. **Artistic Control.** The Illustrator and Publisher shall consult with one another with respect to the title of the Work, the price of the Work, the method and means of advertising and selling the Work, the number and destination of free copies, the number of copies to be printed, the method of printing and other publishing processes, the exact date of publication, the form, style, size, type, paper to be used, and like details, how long the plates or film shall be preserved and when they shall be destroyed, and when new printings of the Work shall be made. In the event of disagreement after consultation, the Publisher shall have final power of decision over all the foregoing matters except the following, which shall be controlled by the Illustrator_____ _____. No changes shall be made in the complete manuscript of the Work by persons other than the Illustrator, except for reasonable copy editing, unless the Illustrator consents to such changes. Publisher shall provide the Illustrator with galleys and proofs which the Illustrator shall review and return to the Publisher within thirty (30) days of receipt. If the cost of the Illustrator's alterations (other than for typesetting errors or unavoidable updating) exceeds _____ percent of the cost of the typography, the Publisher shall have the right to deduct such excess from royalties due Illustrator hereunder.

16. **Original Materials.** Within thirty days after publication, the Publisher shall return the original manuscript and all additional materials to the Illustrator. The Publisher shall provide the Illustrator with a copy of the page proofs, if the Illustrator requests them prior to the date of publication.

17. **Free Copies.** The Illustrator shall receive ____ free copies of the Work as published, after which the Illustrator shall have the right to purchase additional copies at a ____ percent discount from the retail price.

**18. Revisions.** The Illustrator agrees to revise the Work on request by the Publisher. If the Illustrator cannot revise the Work or refuses to do so absent good cause, the Publisher shall have the right to have the Work revised by a person competent to do so and shall charge the costs of said revision against payments due the Illustrator under Paragraph 11 for such revised edition. In no event shall such revision costs exceed $ _____ .

**19. Successors and Assigns.** This Agreement may not be assigned by either party wihout the written consent of the other party hereto. The Illustrator, however, shall retain the right to assign payments due hereunder without obtaining the Publisher's consent. This Agreement shall be binding on the parties and their respective heirs, administrators, successors, and assigns.

**20. Infringement.** In the event of an infringement of the rights granted under this Agreement to the Publisher, the Publisher and the Illustrator shall have the right to sue jointly for the infringement and, after deducting the expenses of bringing suit, to share equally in any recovery. If either party chooses not to join in the suit, the other party may proceed and, after deducting all the expenses of bringing the suit, any recovery shall be shared equally between the parties.

**21. Termination.** The Illustrator shall have the right to terminate this Agreement by written notice if: **(A)** the Work goes out-of-print and the Publisher, within ninety days of receiving notice from the Illustrator that the Work is out-of-print, does not place the Work in print again. A work shall be deemed out-of-print if the work is not available for sale in reasonable quantities in normal trade channels; **(B)** if the Publisher fails to provide statements of account pursuant to Paragraph 10; **(C)** if the Publisher fails to make payments pursuant to Paragraphs 4, 5, 9, or 11; or **(D)** if the Publisher fails to publish in a timely manner pursuant to Paragraph 6. The Publisher shall have the right to terminate this Agreement as provided in Paragraph 3. This Agreement shall automatically terminate in the event of the Publisher's insolvency, bankruptcy, or assignment of assets for the benefit of creditors. In the event of termination of the Agreement, the Publisher shall grant, convey, and transfer all rights in the Work back to the Illustrator.

**22. Production Materials and Unbound Copies.** Upon any termination, the Illustrator may, within sixty days of notification of such termination, purchase the plates, offset negatives, or computer drive tapes (if any) at their scrap value and any remaining copies at the lesser of cost or remainder value.

**23. Promotion.** The Illustrator consents to the use of his or her name, portrait, or picture for promotion and advertising of the Work, provided such use is dignified and consistent with the Illustrator's reputation.

**24. Arbitration.** All disputes arising under this Agreement shall be submitted to binding arbitration before _____ _____ in the following location _____ and shall be settled in accordance with the rules of the American Arbitration Association. Judgment upon the arbitration award may be entered in any court having jurisdiction thereof.

**25. Notice.** Where written notice is required hereunder, it may be given by use of first class mail addressed to the Illustrator or Publisher at the addresses given at the beginning of this Agreement and shall be deemed received five days after mailing. Said addresses for notice may be changed by giving written notice of any new address to the other party.

**26. Modifications in Writing.** All modifications of this Agreement must be in writing and signed by both parties.

**27. Waivers and Defaults**. Any waiver of a breach or default hereunder shall not be deemed a waiver of a subsequent breach or default of either the same provision or any other provision of this Agreement.

**28. Governing Law.** This Agreement shall be governed by the laws of _____ State.

IN WITNESS WHEREOF, the parties have signed this Agreement as of the date first set forth above.

Illustrator_____     Publisher_____
                                                                              Company Name

                                                     By_____
                                                                              Authorized Signatory, Title

# Collaboration Contract

AGREEMENT entered into as of this _____ day of _____, 19___, between _____ (hereinafter referred to as the "Illustrator"), located at _____, and _____ (hereinafter referred to as the "Coauthor"), located at _____.

WHEREAS, each party is familiar with and respects the work of the other; and

WHEREAS, the parties hereto wish to collaborate on a book project tentatively titled _____ _____ (hereinafter referred to as the "Work"); and

WHEREAS, the parties wish to have the creation of the Work governed by the mutual obligations, covenants, and conditions herein;

NOW, THEREFORE, in consideration of the foregoing premises and the mutual covenants hereinafter set forth and other valuable considerations, the parties hereto agree as follows:

1. **Description.** The Work shall be approximately _____ words on the subject of_____ _____ _____ and shall be illustrated by _____ illustrations.
   Materials other than text and illustrations include _____ _____ _____

   A ❑ schedule ❑ outline ❑ synopsis is attached to and made part of this agreement.

2. **Responsibilities.** The Illustrator shall be responsible for creating approximately _____ illustrations to accompany the text, described more fully as follows:

   Subject_____

   Original Size_____

   Reproduction size_____

   Medium_____

   Number and size of color illustrations_____

   Number and size of black and white illustrations_____

   Other specifications_____

   The Illustrator shall also provide the following materials:_____ _____

   The Coauthor shall be responsible for writing approximately _____ words to serve as the following parts of the text: _____ _____

   The Coauthor shall also provide the following materials:_____ _____

3. **Due Date.** Both Illustrator and Coauthor shall complete their portions of the Work by _____, 19 _____, or by the date for delivery of the manuscript as specified in a publishing contract entered into pursuant to Paragraph 4. If such a publishing contract requires sketches or other materials prior to the date for delivery of the manuscript, the party responsible for same shall provide it to the publisher. In the event either party fails to complete his or her portion of the Work by the due date for reasons other than death or disability, the parties may agree to an extension of the due date or agree to allow a nondefaulting party to complete the Work as if the other party were deceased or disabled. If no agreement can be reached, the arbitrator may award a nondefaulting party the right to complete the Work as if the other party were deceased or disabled or may convey to each party the rights of copyright in that party's completed portion of the Work and specify how the parties shall contribute to any expenses incurred and repay any advances.

4. **Contracts and Licenses.** If a contract for the Work has not already been entered into with a publisher, both Illustrator and Coauthor agree to seek such a contract. Such publishing contract shall be entered into in the names of and signed by both the Illustrator and the Coauthor, each of whom shall comply with and perform all required contractual obligations. If a mutually agreeable publishing contract for initial publication of the Work is not entered into with a Publisher by _____, 19_____, then either party may terminate this agreement by giving written notice to the other party prior to such time as a mutually agreeable publishing contract for initial publication is entered into. Each party shall fully inform the other party of all negotiations for such a publishing contract or with respect to the negotiation of any other licenses or contracts pursuant to this Agreement. The disposition of any right, including the grant of any license, shall require written agreement between both parties hereto. Each party shall receive a copy of any contract, license, or other document relating to this Agreement.

5. **Copyright, Trademarks, and Other Proprietary Rights.** Illustrator and Coauthor agree that the Work shall be copyrighted in both their names, and that upon completion of the Work it is their intention that their respective contributions shall be merged into a joint work with a jointly owned copyright, unless provided to the contrary here:_____. If either party does not complete their portion of the Work, the nature of copyright ownership shall be governed by Paragraph 3. It is further agreed that trademarks, rights in characters, titles, and similar ongoing rights shall be owned by both parties who shall both participate in any sequels under the terms of this Agreement, unless provided to the contrary here:_____. A sequel is defined as a work closely related to the Work in that it is derived from the subject matter of the Work, is similar in style and format to the Work, and is directed toward the same audience as that for the Work. Material of any and all kinds developed or obtained in the course of creating the work shall be ❑ jointly owned ❑ the property of the party who developed or obtained it.

6. **Income and Expenses.** Net proceeds generated by the Work shall be divided as set forth in this Paragraph. Net proceeds are defined as gross proceeds from the sale or license of book rights throughout the world (including but not limited to serializations, condensations, and translations), including advances, minus reasonable expenses. Such expenses shall include agents' fees and the parties' expenses incurred in the creation of the Work, provided that the parties' expenses shall be supported by appropriate verification and shall not exceed $_____ for the Illustrator and $_____ for the Coauthor. Each party shall provide verification for expenses to the other party within ten days of a written request. Unless otherwise provided, the parties' expenses shall be reimbursed from first proceeds received, including but not limited to advances.

Net proceeds from the sale or license of publishing rights shall be divided _____ percent to the Illustrator and _____ percent to the Coauthor.

Net proceeds from the sale or license of nonpublishing rights in the Work (including but not limited to audio, merchandising, motion picture, stage play, or television rights to the Work), whether such sale or license occurs before or after initial publication of the Work, shall be divided _____ percent to the Illustrator and _____ percent to the Coauthor, unless provided to the contrary here, in which case the following rights shall be treated with respect to division of net proceeds and control or disposition as follows:_____ _____.

If possible, net proceeds shall be paid directly to each party in accordance with the divisions set forth in this Paragraph. If either party is designated to collect such net proceeds, that party shall make immediate payment to the other party of such amounts as are due hereunder.

7. **Agent.** If the parties have entered into an agency agreement with respect to the Work, it is with the following agent:_____. If a contract for the Work has not already been entered into with an agent, both Illustrator and Coauthor agree ❏ to seek such a contract ❏ not to seek such a contract. Any agency contract shall be mutually acceptable to and entered into in the names of and signed by both the Illustrator and the Coauthor, each of whom shall comply with and perform all required contractual obligations.

8. **Authorship Credit.** The credit line for the Work shall be as follows wherever authorship credit is given in the Work or in promotion, advertising, or other ancillary uses:_____ _____. The color and type size for such authorship credit shall be the same for both authors unless provided to the contrary here:_____ _____.

9. **Artistic Control.** Each party shall have artistic control over his or his portion of the Work, unless provided to the contrary here in which case artistic control of the entire Work shall be exercised by _____ _____. The parties shall share ideas and make their work in progress available to the other party for discussion and coordination purposes. Except as provided in Paragraphs 3 and 12, neither party shall at any time make any changes in the portion of the Work created by the other party.

10. **Warranty and Indemnity.** Illustrator and Coauthor each warrant and represent to the other that the respective contributions of each to the Work are original (or that appropriate releases have been obtained and paid for) and do not libel or otherwise violate any right of any person or entity, including but not limited to rights of copyright or privacy. Illustrator and Coauthor each indemnify and hold the other harmless from and against any and all claims, actions, liability, damages, costs, and expenses, including reasonable legal fees and expenses, incurred by the other as a result of the breach of such warranties, representations, and undertakings.

11. **Assignment.** This Agreement shall not be assignable by either party hereto, provided, however, that after completion of the Work, either party may assign the right to receive money pursuant to Paragraph 6 by giving written notice to the other party.

12. **Death or Disability.** In the event that either party dies or suffers a disability that will prevent completion of his or her respective portion of the Work, or of a revision thereof or a sequel thereto, the other party shall have the right to complete that portion or to hire a third party to complete that portion and shall adjust the authorship credit to reflect the revised authorship arrangements. The deceased or disabled party shall receive payments pursuant to Paragraph 6 pro rata to the proportion of his or her work completed or, in the case of a revision or sequel, shall receive payments pursuant to Paragraph 6 after deduction for the cost of revising or creating the sequel with respect to his or her portion of the Work. The active party shall have the sole power to license

and contract with respect to the Work, and approval of the personal representative, heirs, or conservator of the deceased or disabled party shall not be required. If all parties are deceased, the respective heirs or personal representatives shall take the place of the parties for all purposes.

**13. Arbitration.** All disputes arising under this Agreement shall be submitted to binding arbitration before _____ in the following location _____ and shall be settled in accordance with the rules of the American Arbitration Association. Judgment upon the arbitration award may be entered in any court having jurisdiction thereof.

**14. Term.** The term for this Agreement shall be the duration of the copyright, plus any renewals or extensions thereof.

**15. Independent Parties.** The parties to this Agreement are independent of one another, and nothing contained in this Agreement shall make a partnership or joint venture between them.

**16. Competitive Works.** If the parties wish to restrict future activities to avoid competition with the Work, any such restrictions must be stated here: _____

_____

**17. Infringement.** In the event of an infringement of the Work, the Illustrator and Coauthor shall have the right to sue jointly for the infringement and, after deducting the expenses of bringing suit, to share in any recovery as follows:_____. If either party chooses not to join in the suit, the other party may proceed and, after deducting all the expenses of bringing the suit, any recovery shall be shared between the parties as stated in the preceding sentence.

**18. Miscellany.** This Agreement shall be binding upon the parties hereto, their heirs, successors, assigns, and personal representatives. This Agreement constitutes the entire understanding between the parties. Its terms can be modified only by an instrument in writing signed by both parties. Each party shall do all acts and sign all documents required to effectuate this Agreement. A waiver of any breach of any of the provisions of this Agreement shall not be construed as a continuing waiver of other breaches of the same or other provisions hereof. This Agreement shall be governed by the laws of the State of _____.

IN WITNESS WHEREOF, the parties hereto have signed this Agreement as of the date first set forth above.

Illustrator_____     Coauthor_____

# Contract for the Sale of an Artwork

AGREEMENT made as of the _____ day of _____, 19_____, between _____ (hereinafter referred to as the "Illustrator"), located at _____ _____, and _____ (hereinafter referred to as the "Collector"), located at _____, with respect to the sale of an artwork (hereinafter referred to as the "Work").

WHEREAS, the Illustrator has created the Work and has full right, title, and interest therein; and
WHEREAS, the Illustrator wishes to sell the Work; and
WHEREAS, the Collector has viewed the Work and wishes to purchase it;
NOW, THEREFORE, in consideration of the foregoing premises and the mutual obligations, covenants, and conditions hereinafter set forth, and other valuable considerations, the parties hereto agree as follows:

**1. Description of Work.** The Illustrator describes the Work as follows:

Title: _____

Medium: _____

Size: _____

Framing or Mounting: _____

Year of Creation: _____

Signed by Illustrator:   ❑ Yes   ❑ No

If the Work is part of a limited edition, indicate the method of production _____; the size of the edition_____; how many multiples are signed_____; how many are unsigned_____; how many are numbered_____; how many are unnumbered_____; how many proofs exist_____; the quantity of any prior editions_____; and whether the master image has been cancelled or destroyed   ❑ yes   ❑ no.

**2. Sale.** The Illustrator hereby agrees to sell the Work to the Collector. Title shall pass to the Collector at such time as full payment is received by the Illustrator pursuant to Paragraph 4 hereof.

**3. Price.** The Collector agrees to purchase the Work for the agreed upon price of $_____, and shall also pay any applicable sales or transfer taxes.

**4. Payment.** Payment shall be made in full upon the signing of this Agreement.

**5. Delivery.** The ❑ Illustrator ❑ Collector shall arrange for delivery to the following location:_____ _____ no later than _____, 19____. The expenses of delivery (including, but not limited to, insurance and transportation) shall be paid by _____.

**6. Risk of Loss and Insurance.** The risk of loss or damage to the Work and the provision of any insurance to cover such loss or damage shall be the responsibility of the Collector from the time of_____ _____.

**7. Copyright and Reproduction.** The Illustrator reserves all reproduction rights, including the right to claim statutory copyright, in the Work. The Work may not be photographed, sketched, painted, or reproduced in any manner whatsoever without the express, written consent of the Illustrator. All approved reproductions shall bear the following copyright notice: © by (Illustrator's name) 19____.

**8. Miscellany.** This Agreement shall be binding upon the parties hereto, their heirs, successors, assigns, and personal representatives. This Agreement constitutes the entire understanding between the parties. Its terms can be modified only by an instrument in writing signed by both parties. A waiver of any breach of any of the provisions of this Agreement shall not be construed as a continuing waiver of other breaches of the same or other provisions hereof. This Agreement shall be governed by the laws of the State of _____.

IN WITNESS WHEREOF, the parties hereto have signed this Agreement as of the date first set forth above.

Illustrator _____ Collector _____

# Contract for Receipt and Holding of Artwork

AGREEMENT entered into as of this _____ day of _____, 19____, between _____ (hereinafter referred to as the "Illustrator"), located at_____., and

_____ (hereinafter referred to as the "Recipient"), located at_____.

WHEREAS, the Illustrator is a professional illustrator of good standing; and

WHEREAS, the Illustrator wishes to leave certain artworks with the Recipient for a limited period of time; and

WHEREAS, the Recipient in the course of its business receives and holds artworks;

NOW, THEREFORE, in consideration of the foregoing premises and the mutual covenants hereinafter set forth and other valuable consideration, the parties hereto agree as follows:

1. **Purpose.** Illustrator hereby agrees to entrust the artworks listed on the Schedule of Artworks to the Recipient for the purpose of: _____

2. **Acceptance.** Recipient accepts the listing and values on the Schedule of Artworks as accurate if not objected to in writing by return mail immediately after receipt of the artworks. If Recipient has not signed this form, any terms on this form not objected to in writing within 10 days shall be deemed accepted.

3. **Ownership and Copyright.** Copyright and all reproduction rights in the artworks, as well as the ownership of the physical artworks themselves, are the property of and reserved to the Illustrator. Recipient acknowledges that the artworks shall be held in confidence and agrees not to display, copy, or modify directly or indirectly any of the artworks submitted, nor will Recipient permit any third party to do any of the foregoing. Reproduction, display, sale, or rental shall be allowed only upon Illustrator's written permission specifying usage and fees.

4. **Loss, Theft, or Damage.** Recipient agrees to assume full responsibility and be strictly liable for loss, theft, or damage to the artworks from the time of ❑ shipment by the Illustrator ❑ receipt by the Recipient until the time of ❑ shipment by the Recipient ❑ receipt by the Illustrator. Recipient further agrees to return all of the artworks at its own expense by the following method of transportation: _____.
   Reimbursement for loss, theft, or damage to an artwork shall be in the amount of the value entered for that artwork on the Schedule of Artworks. Both Recipient and Illustrator agree that the specified values represent the value of the art.

5. **Insurance.** Recipient ❑ does ❑ does not agree to insure the artworks for all risks from the time of shipment from the artist until the time of delivery to the artist for the values shown on the Schedule of Artworks.

6. **Holding Fees.** The artworks are to be returned to the Illustrator within _____ days after delivery to the Recipient. Each artwork held beyond _____ days from delivery shall incur the following daily holding fee: $_____ which shall be paid to the Illustrator on a weekly basis.

7. **Arbitration.** Recipient and Illustrator agree to submit all disputes hereunder in excess of $_____ to arbitration before _____ at the following location _____ under the rules of the American Arbitration Association. The arbitrator's award shall be final and judgment may be entered on it in any court having jurisdiction thereof.

8. **Miscellany.** This Agreement contains the full understanding between the parties hereto and may only be modified by a written instrument signed by both parties. It shall be governed by the laws of the state of _____.

IN WITNESS WHEREOF, the parties hereto have signed this Agreement as of the date first set forth above.

Illustrator_____    Recipient_____

Company Name

By_____

Authorized Signatory, Title

## Schedule of Artworks

| | Title | Medium | Description | Framing | Value |
|---|---|---|---|---|---|
| 1. | | | | | |
| 2. | | | | | |
| 3. | | | | | |
| 4. | | | | | |
| 5. | | | | | |
| 6. | | | | | |
| 7. | | | | | |
| 8. | | | | | |
| 9. | | | | | |
| 10. | | | | | |
| 11. | | | | | |
| 12. | | | | | |
| 13. | | | | | |
| 14. | | | | | |
| 15. | | | | | |

# Illustrator—Gallery Contract with Record of Consignment and Statement of Account

AGREEMENT entered into as of this _____ day of _____, 19____, between_____ (hereinafter referred to as the "Illustrator"), located at _____, and _____ (hereinafter referred to as the "Gallery"), located at _____.

WHEREAS, the Illustrator is a professional illustrator of good standing; and

WHEREAS, the Illustrator wishes to have certain artworks represented by the Gallery, and

WHEREAS, the Gallery wishes to represent the Illustrator under the terms and conditions of this Agreement,

NOW, THEREFORE, in consideration of the foregoing premises and the mutual covenants hereinafter set forth and other valuable consideration, the parties hereto agree as follows:

1. **Scope of Agency.** The Illustrator appoints the Gallery to act as Illustrator's ❑ exclusive ❑ nonexclusive agent in the following geographic area:_____ for the exhibition and sales of artworks in the following media: _____. This agency shall cover only artwork completed by the Illustrator while this Agreement is in force. The Gallery shall document receipt of all works consigned hereunder by signing and returning to the Illustrator a Record of Consignment in the form annexed to this contract as Appendix A.

2. **Term and Termination.** This Agreement shall have a term of _____ years and may be terminated by either party giving sixty days written notice to the other party. The Agreement shall automatically terminate with the death of the Illustrator, the death or termination of employment of _____ with the Gallery, if the Gallery moves outside of the area of _____, or if the Gallery becomes bankrupt or insolvent. On termination, all works consigned hereunder shall immediately be returned to the Illustrator at the expense of the Gallery.

3. **Exhibitions.** The Gallery shall provide a solo exhibition for the Illustrator of _____ days between _____ and _____ in the exhibition space located at _____ which shall be exclusively devoted to the Illustrator's exhibition for the specified time period. The Illustrator shall have artistic control over the exhibition of his or her work and the quality of reproduction of such work for promotional or advertising purposes. The expenses of the exhibition shall be paid for in the respective percentages shown below:

| Exhibition Expenses | Illustrator | Gallery |
|---|---|---|
| Transporting work to gallery (including insurance and packing).............. | _____ | _____ |
| Advertising......................................................................... | _____ | _____ |
| Catalogs............................................................................ | _____ | _____ |
| Announcements.................................................................... | _____ | _____ |
| Frames............................................................................... | _____ | _____ |
| Special installations............................................................. | _____ | _____ |
| Photographing work.............................................................. | _____ | _____ |
| Party for opening................................................................. | _____ | _____ |
| Shipping to purchasers.......................................................... | _____ | _____ |
| Transporting work back to illustrator (including insurance and packing) | _____ | _____ |
| All other expenses arising from the exhibition................................. | _____ | _____ |

No expense which is to be shared shall be incurred by either party without the prior written consent of the other party as to the amount of the expense. After the exhibition, the frames, photographs, negatives, and any other tangible property created in the course of the exhibition shall be the property of _____.

4. **Commissions**. The Gallery shall receive a commission of ____ percent of the retail price of each work sold. In the case of discount sales, the discount shall be deducted from the Gallery's commission. If the Gallery's agency is exclusive, then the Gallery shall receive a commission of _____ percent of the retail price for each studio sale by the Illustrator that falls within the scope of the Gallery's exclusivity. Works done on a commissioned basis by the Illustrator ❑ shall ❑ shall not be considered studio sales on which the Gallery may be entitled to a commission.

5. **Prices**. The Gallery shall sell the works at the retail prices shown on the Record of Consignment, subject to the Gallery's right to make customary trade discounts to such purchasers as museums and designers.

6. **Payments**. The Gallery shall pay the Illustrator all proceeds due to the Illustrator within thirty days of sale. No sales on approval or credit shall be made without the Illustrator's written consent and, in such cases, the first proceeds received by the Gallery shall be paid to the Illustrator until the Illustrator has been paid all proceeds due.

7. **Accounting**. The Gallery shall furnish the Illustrator with an accounting every _____ months in the form attached hereto as Appendix B, the first such accounting to be given on the first day of _____, 19____. Each accounting shall state for each work sold during the accounting period the following information: the title of the work, the date of sale, the sale price, the name and address of the purchaser, the amounts due the Gallery and the Illustrator, and the location of all works consigned to the Gallery that have not been sold. An accounting shall be provided in the event of termination of this Agreement.

8. **Inspection of Books**. The Gallery shall maintain accurate books and documentation with respect to all transactions entered into for the Illustrator. On the Illustrator's written request, the Gallery will permit the Illustrator or the Illustrator's authorized representative to examine these books and documentation during normal business hours of the Gallery.

9. **Loss or Damage**. The Gallery shall be responsible for the safekeeping of all consigned artworks. The Gallery shall be strictly liable for loss or damage to any consigned artwork from the date of delivery to the Gallery until the work is returned to the Illustrator or delivered to a purchaser. In the event of loss or damage that cannot be restored, the Illustrator shall receive the same amount as if the work had been sold at the retail price listed in the Record of Consignment. If restoration is undertaken, the Illustrator shall have a veto power over the choice of the restorer.

10. **Insurance**. The Gallery shall insure the work for ____ percent of the retail price shown in the Record of Consignment.

11. **Copyright**. The Gallery shall take all steps necessary to insure that the Illustrator's copyright in the consigned works is protected, including but not limited to requiring copyright notices on all reproductions of the works used for any purpose whatsoever.

12. **Security Interest**. Title to and a security interest in any works consigned or proceeds of sale under this Agreement are reserved to the Illustrator. In the event of any default by the Gallery, the Illustrator shall have all the rights of a secured party under the Uniform Commercial Code and the works shall not be subject to claims by the Gallery's creditors. The Gallery agrees to execute and deliver to the Illustrator, in the form requested by the Illustrator, a financing statement and such other documents which the Illustrator may require to perfect its security interest in the works. In the event of the purchase of any work by a party other than the Gallery, title shall pass directly from the Illustrator to the other party. In the event of the purchase of any work by the Gallery, title

shall pass only upon full payment to the Illustrator of all sums due hereunder. The Gallery agrees not to pledge or encumber any works in its possession, nor to incur any charge or obligation in connection therewith for which the Illustrator may be liable.

**13. Assignment.** This Agreement shall not be assignable by either party hereto, provided, however, that the Illustrator shall have the right to assign money due him or her hereunder.

**14. Arbitration.** All disputes arising under this Agreement shall be submitted to binding arbitration before _____ in the following location _____ and the arbitration award may be entered for judgement in any court having jurisdiction thereof. Notwithstanding the foregoing, either party may refuse to arbitrate when the dispute is for a sum of less than $_____.

**15. Modifications.** All modifications of this Agreement must be in writing and signed by both parties. This Agreement constitutes the entire understanding between the parties hereto.

**16. Governing Law.** This Agreement shall be governed by the laws of the State of _____.

IN WITNESS WHEREOF, the parties hereto have signed this Agreement as of the date first set forth above.


Illustrator_____      Gallery_____
                                                                                    Company Name


                                                                  By_____
                                                                                    Authorized Signatory, Title

## APPENDIX A:    Record of Consignment

This is to acknowledge receipt of the following works of art on consignment:

| Title | Medium | Description | Retail Price |
|---|---|---|---|
| 1. | | | |
| 2. | | | |
| 3. | | | |
| 4. | | | |
| 5. | | | |
| 6. | | | |
| 7. | | | |
| 8. | | | |
| 9. | | | |


Gallery _____
                        Company Name


By _____
                    Authorized Signatory, Title

**APPENDIX B:    Statement of Account**

Date: _____, 19_____

Acounting for Period from _____, 19_____, through _____, 19_____.

The following works were sold during this period:

| Title | Date Sold | Purchaser's Name and Address | Sale Price | Gallery's Commission | Due Illustrator |
|---|---|---|---|---|---|
| 1._____ | ____ | _____ | _____ | _____ | _____ |
| _____ | ____ | _____ | _____ | _____ | _____ |
| 2._____ | ____ | _____ | _____ | _____ | _____ |
| _____ | ____ | _____ | _____ | _____ | _____ |
| 3._____ | ____ | _____ | _____ | _____ | _____ |
| _____ | ____ | _____ | _____ | _____ | _____ |
| 4._____ | ____ | _____ | _____ | _____ | _____ |
| _____ | ____ | _____ | _____ | _____ | _____ |

The total due you of $_____ is enclosed with this Statement of Account.

The following works remain on consignment with the gallery:

| Title | Location |
|---|---|
| 1._____ | _____ |
| 2._____ | _____ |
| 3._____ | _____ |
| 4._____ | _____ |
| 5._____ | _____ |
| 6._____ | _____ |
| 7._____ | _____ |
| 8._____ | _____ |
| 9._____ | _____ |

Gallery _____
                               Company Name

By _____
                        Authorized Signatory, Title

# Illustrator's Lecture Contract

AGREEMENT, dated the _____ day of _____, 19 ____, between_____
(hereinafter referred to as the "Illustrator"), located at _____and
_____(hereinafter referred to as the "Sponsor"),
located at _____.

WHEREAS, the Sponsor is familiar with and admires the work of the Illustrator; and

WHEREAS, the Sponsor wishes the Illustrator to visit the Sponsor to enhance the opportunities for its students to have contact with working professional illustrator; and

WHEREAS, the Illustrator wishes to lecture with respect to his or her work and perform such other services as this contract may call for;

NOW, THEREFORE, in consideration of the foregoing premises and the mutual covenants hereinafter set forth and other valuable considerations, the parties hereto agree as follows:

1. **Illustrator to Lecture.** The Illustrator hereby agrees to come to the Sponsor on the following date(s):_____
   _____ and perform the following services:
   _____.

   The Illustrator shall use best efforts to make his or her services as productive as possible to the Sponsor. The Illustrator further agrees to bring examples of his or her own work in the form of _____
   _____.

2. **Payment.** The Sponsor agrees to pay as full compensation for the Illustrator's services rendered under Paragraph 1 the sum of $_____. This sum shall be payable to the Illustrator on completion of the _____ day of the Illustrator's residence with the Sponsor.

3. **Expenses.** In addition to the payments provided under Paragraph 2, the Sponsor agrees to reimburse the Illustrator for the following expenses:

   **(A)** Travel expenses in the amount of $_____.

   **(B)** Food and lodging expenses in the amount of $_____.

   **(C)** Other expenses listed here:_____in the amount of $_____.

   The reimbursement for travel expenses shall be made fourteen (14 days prior to the earliest date specified in Paragraph 1). The reimbursement for food, lodging, and other expenses shall be made at the date of payment specified in Paragraph 2, unless a contrary date is specified here:_____.

   In addition, the Sponsor shall provide the Illustrator with the following:

   **(A)** Tickets for travel, rental car, or other modes of transportation as follows: _____
   _____

   **(B)** Food and lodging as follows: _____
   _____

   **(C)** Other hospitality as follows: _____
   _____

4. **Inability to Perform.** If the Illustrator is unable to appear on the dates scheduled in Paragraph 1 due to illness, the Sponsor shall have no obligation to make any payments under Paragraphs 2 and 3, but shall attempt to reschedule the Illustrator's appearance at a mutually acceptable future date. If the Sponsor is prevented from

having the Illustrator appear by Acts of God, hurricane, flood, governmental order, or other cause beyond its control, the Sponsor shall be responsible only for the payment of such expenses under Paragraph 3 as the Illustrator shall have actually incurred. The Sponsor agrees in such a case to attempt to reschedule the Illustrator's appearance at a mutually acceptable future date.

5. **Late Payment.** The Sponsor agrees that, in the event it is late in making payment of amounts due to the Illustrator under Paragraphs 2, 3, or 8, it will pay as additional liquidated damages _____ percent in interest on the amounts it is owing to the Author, said interest to run from the date stipulated for payment in Paragraphs 2, 3, or 8 until such time as payment is made.

6. **Copyrights and Recordings.** Both parties agree that the Illustrator shall retain all rights, including copyrights, in relation to recordings of any kind made of the appearance or any works shown in the course thereof. The term "recording" as used herein shall include any recording made by electrical transcription, tape recording, wire recording, film, videotape, or other similar or dissimilar method of recording, whether now known or hereinafter developed. No use of any such recording shall be made by the Sponsor without the written consent of the Author and, if stipulated therein, additional compensation for such use.

7. **Insurance and Loss or Damage.** The sponsor agrees that it shall provide wall-to-wall insurance for the works listed on the Schedule of Art Works for the values specified therein. The Sponsor agrees that it shall be fully responsible and have strict liability for any loss or damage to the artwork from the time said artwork leaves the Illustrator's residence or studio until such time as it is returned there.

8. **Packing and Shipping.** The Sponsor agrees that it shall fully bear any costs of packing and shipping necessary to deliver the works specified in Paragraph 7 to the Sponsor and return them to the Illustrator's residence or studio.

9. **Modification.** This contract contains the full understanding between the parties hereto and may only be modified in a written instrument signed by both parties.

10. **Governing Law.** This contract shall be governed by the laws of the State of _____.

IN WITNESS WHEREOF, the parties hereto have signed this Agreement as of the date first set forth above.

Author_____     Sponsor_____
                                                                                    Company Name

                                                              By_____
                                                                             Authorized Signatory, Title

**Schedule of Artworks**

| Title | Medium | Size | Value |
|---|---|---|---|
| 1._____ | _____ | _____ | _____ |
| 2._____ | _____ | _____ | _____ |
| 3._____ | _____ | _____ | _____ |
| 4._____ | _____ | _____ | _____ |
| 5._____ | _____ | _____ | _____ |
| 6._____ | _____ | _____ | _____ |
| 7._____ | _____ | _____ | _____ |

# Licensing Contract to Merchandise Images

AGREEMENT made this _____ day of _____, 19_____, between _____
(hereinafter referred to as the "Illustrator"), located at _____
and _____ (hereinafter referred to as the "Licensee"),
located at _____
with respect to the use of a certain image created by the Illustrator (hereinafter referred to as the "Image") for
manufactured products (hereinafter referred to as the "Licensed Products").

WHEREAS, the Illustrator is a professional illustrator of good standing; and

WHEREAS, the Illustrator has created the Image which the Illustrator wishes to license for purposes of manufacture
and sale; and

WHEREAS, the Licensee wishes to use the Image to create a certain product or products for manufacture and sale;
and

WHEREAS, both parties want to achieve the best possible quality to generate maximum sales;

NOW, THEREFORE, in consideration of the foregoing premises and the mutual covenants hereinafter set forth and
other valuable consideration, the parties hereto agree as follows:

1. **Grant of Merchandising Rights.** The Illustrator grants to the Licensee the ❑ exclusive ❑ nonexclusive right
   to use the Image, titled _____ and described as
   _____, which was created and
   is owned by the Illustrator, as or as part of the following type(s) of merchandise:_____
   _____
   for manufacture, distribution, and sale by the Licensee in the following geographical area:_____
   _____ and for the following period of time:
   _____.

2. **Ownership of Copyright.** The Illustrator shall retain all copyrights in and to the Image. The Licensee shall identify
   the Illustrator as the creator of the Image on the Licensed Products and shall reproduce thereon a copyright notice
   for the Illustrator which shall include the word "Copyright" or the symbol for copyright, the Illustrator's name, and
   the year date of first publication.

3. **Advance and Royalties.** Licensee agrees to pay Illustrator a nonrefundable advance in the amount of
   $_____ upon signing this Agreement, which advance shall be recouped from first royalties due hereunder.
   Licensee further agrees to pay Illustrator a royalty of _____ ( _____ %) percent of the net sales of the Licensed
   Products. "Net Sales" as used herein shall mean sales to customers less prepaid freight and credits for lawful and
   customary volume rebates, actual returns, and allowances. Royalties shall be deemed to accrue when the
   Licensed Products are sold, shipped, or invoiced, whichever first occurs.

4. **Payments and Statements of Account.** Royalty payments shall be paid monthly on the first day of each month
   commencing _____, 19 _____, and Licensee shall with each payment furnish Illustrator with a monthly
   statement of account showing the kinds and quantities of all Licensed Products sold, the prices received therefor,
   and all deductions for freight, volume rebates, returns, and allowances. The Illustrator shall have the right to
   terminate this Agreement upon thirty (30) days notice if Licensee fails to make any payment required of it and does
   not cure this default within said thirty (30) days, whereupon all rights granted herein shall revert immediately to
   the Illustrator.

5. **Inspection of Books and Records.** Illustrator shall have the right to inspect Licensee's books and records
   concerning sales of the Licensed Products upon prior written notice.

**6. Samples.** Licensee shall give the Illustrator _____ samples of the Licensed Products for the Illustrator's personal use. The Illustrator shall have the right to purchase additional samples of the Licensed Products at the Licensee's manufacturing cost.

**7. Quality of Reproductions.** The Illustrator shall have the right to approve the quality of the reproduction of the Image on the Licensed Products, and the Illustrator agrees not to withhold approval unreasonably.

**8. Promotion.** Licensee shall use its best efforts to promote, distribute, and sell the Licensed Products.

**9. Reservation of Rights.** All rights not specifically transferred by this Agreement are reserved to the Illustrator.

**10. Indemnification.** The Licensee shall hold the Illustrator harmless from and against any loss, expense, or damage occasioned by any claim, demand, suit, or recovery against the Illustrator arising out of the use of the Image for the Licensed Products.

**11. Assignment.** Neither party shall assign rights or obligations under this Agreement, except that the Illustrator may assign the right to receive money due hereunder.

**12. Nature of Contract.** Nothing herein shall be construed to constitute the parties hereto joint venturers, nor shall any similar relationship be deemed to exist between them.

**13. Governing Law.** This Agreement shall be construed in accordance with the laws of _____, Licensee consents to the jurisdiction of the courts of _____.

**14. Addresses.** All notices, demands, payments, royalty payments, and statements shall be sent to the Illustrator at the following address _____ and to the Licensee at _____.

**15. Modifications in Writing.** This Agreement constitutes the entire agreement between the parties hereto and shall not be modified, amended, or changed in any way except by a written agreement signed by both parties hereto.


IN WITNESS WHEREOF, the parties have signed this Agreement as of the date first set forth above.


Illustrator_____     Licensee_____
                                                                   Company Name


                                                 By_____
                                                      Authorized Signatory, Title

# Release Form for Models

In consideration of _____ Dollars ($_____ ), receipt

of which is acknowledged, I, _____ , do hereby give _____ ,

his or her assigns, licensees, and legal representatives the irrevocable right to use my name (or any fictional name), picture, portrait, or photograph in all forms and media and in all manners, including composite or distorted representations, for advertising, trade, or any other lawful purposes, and I waive any right to inspect or approve the finished version(s), including written copy that may be created in connection therewith. I am of full age.* I have read this release and am fully familiar with its contents.

Witness_____    Model_____

Address_____    Address_____

Date _____, 19 ___

_____    **Consent (if applicable)**    _____

I am the parent or guardian of the minor named above and have the legal authority to execute the above release. I approve the foregoing and waive any rights in the premises.

Witness_____    Parent or Guardian_____

Address_____    Address_____

Date _____, 19 ____

* Delete this sentence if the subject is a minor.  The parent or guardian must then sign the consent.

# Property Release

In consideration of the sum of _____Dollars ($_____),

receipt of which is hereby acknowledged, I, _____,

located at _____, do irrevocably authorize

_____, his or her assigns, licensees, heirs, and legal representatives, to copyright, publish, and use in all forms and media and in all manners for advertising, trade, or any other lawful purpose, images of the following property which I own and have full and sole authority to license for such uses: _____
_____,

regardless of whether said use is composite or distorted in character or form, whether said use is made in conjunction with my own name or with a fictitious name, or whether said use is made in color or otherwise or other derivative works are made through any medium.

I waive any right that I may have to inspect or approve the finished version(s), including written copy that may be used in connection therewith.

I am of full age and have every right to contract in my own name with respect to the foregoing matters. I have read the above authorization and release prior to its execution and I am fully cognizant of its contents.


Witness_____     Owner_____


Address_____     Date _____, 19_____

# Permission Form

The Undersigned hereby grant(s) permission to _____ (hereinafter

referred to as the "Illustrator"), located at _____,

and to the Illustrator's successors and assigns, to use the material specified in this Permission Form in the book

titled _____ to be

published by _____.

This permission is for the following material:

Nature of material _____

Source _____

Exact description of material, including page numbers_____

If published, date of publication _____

Publisher _____

Author(s) _____

This material may be used in the Illustrator's book and in any future revisions and editions thereof, including nonexclusive world rights in all languages.

It is understood that the grant of this permission shall in no way restrict republication of the material by the Undersigned or others authorized by the Undersigned.

If specified here, the material shall be accompanied on publication by a copyright notice as follows_____
_____

and a credit line as follows _____.

Other provisions, if any: _____

If specified here, the requested rights are not controlled in their entirety by the Undersigned and the following owners
must be contacted: _____
_____

One copy of this Permission Form shall be returned to the Illustrator and one copy shall be retained by the Undersigned.

_____          _____
Authorized Signatory                                          Date

_____          _____
Authorized Signatory                                          Date

# Nondisclosure Agreement for Submitting Ideas

AGREEMENT, entered into as of this _____ day of _____, 19___, between_____ (hereinafter referred to as the "Illustrator"), located at _____, and _____ (hereinafter referred to as the "Recipient"), located at _____.

WHEREAS, the Illustrator has developed certain valuable information, concepts, ideas, or designs, which the Illustrator deems confidential (hereinafter referred to as the "Information"); and

WHEREAS, the Recipient is in the business of using such Information for its projects and wishes to review the Information; and

WHEREAS, the Illustrator wishes to disclose this Information to the Recipient; and

WHEREAS, the Recipient is willing not to disclose this Information, as provided in this Agreement.

NOW, THEREFORE, in consideration of the foregoing premises and the mutual covenants hereinafter set forth and other valuable considerations, the parties hereto agree as follows:

1. **Disclosure.** Illustrator shall disclose to the Recipient the Information, which concerns:_____ _____

2. **Purpose.** Recipient agrees that this disclosure is only for the purpose of the Recipient's evaluation to determine its interest in the commercial exploitation of the Information.

3. **Limitation on Use.** Recipient agrees not to manufacture, sell, deal in, or otherwise use or appropriate the disclosed Information in any way whatsoever, including but not limited to adaptation, imitation, redesign, or modification. Nothing contained in this Agreement shall be deemed to give Recipient any rights whatsoever in and to the Information.

4. **Confidentiality.** Recipient understands and agrees that the unauthorized disclosure of the Information by the Recipient to others would irreparably damage the Illustrator. As consideration and in return for the disclosure of this Information, the Recipient shall keep secret and hold in confidence all such Information and treat the Information as if it were the Recipient's own proprietary property by not disclosing it to any person or entity.

5. **Good Faith Negotiations.** If, on the basis of the evaluation of the Information, Recipient wishes to pursue the exploitation thereof, Recipient agrees to enter into good faith negotiations to arrive at a mutually satisfactory agreement for these purposes. Until and unless such an agreement is entered into, this nondisclosure Agreement shall remain in force.

6. **Miscellany.** This Agreement shall be binding upon and shall inure to the benefit of the parties and their respective legal representatives, successors, and assigns.

IN WITNESS WHEREOF, the parties have signed this Agreement as of the date first set forth above.


Illustrator_____     Recipient_____
                                                                       Company Name


                                                  By_____
                                                                  Authorized Signatory, Title

# Copyright Transfer Form

FOR VALUABLE CONSIDERATION, the receipt of which is hereby acknowledged, _____

(hereinafter referred to as the "Assignor"), located at _____,

does hereby transfer and assign to _____, located

at _____, his or her heirs, executors, administrators,

and assigns, the following rights: _____

_____ in the copyrights

in the works described as follows:

| Title | Registration Number | Nature of Work |
|-------|---------------------|----------------|
| _____ | _____ | _____ |
| _____ | _____ | _____ |
| _____ | _____ | _____ |
| _____ | _____ | _____ |
| _____ | _____ | _____ |

IN WITNESS WHEREOF, the Assignor has executed this instrument on the _____ day of _____, 19___.

Assignor_____

# FORM VA
## UNITED STATES COPYRIGHT OFFICE

REGISTRATION NUMBER

VA          VAU

EFFECTIVE DATE OF REGISTRATION

Month      Day      Year

**DO NOT WRITE ABOVE THIS LINE. IF YOU NEED MORE SPACE, USE A SEPARATE CONTINUATION SHEET.**

## 1

**TITLE OF THIS WORK** ▼          **NATURE OF THIS WORK** ▼ See instructions

**PREVIOUS OR ALTERNATIVE TITLES** ▼

**PUBLICATION AS A CONTRIBUTION** If this work was published as a contribution to a periodical, serial, or collection, give information about the collective work in which the contribution appeared. **Title of Collective Work** ▼

If published in a periodical or serial give: **Volume** ▼      **Number** ▼      **Issue Date** ▼      **On Pages** ▼

## 2

### a

**NAME OF AUTHOR** ▼          **DATES OF BIRTH AND DEATH**
Year Born ▼      Year Died ▼

Was this contribution to the work a "work made for hire"?
☐ Yes
☐ No

**AUTHOR'S NATIONALITY OR DOMICILE**
Name of Country
OR { Citizen of ▶_____
Domiciled in ▶_____

**WAS THIS AUTHOR'S CONTRIBUTION TO THE WORK**
Anonymous? ☐ Yes ☐ No
Pseudonymous? ☐ Yes ☐ No
If the answer to either of these questions is "Yes," see detailed instructions.

**NATURE OF AUTHORSHIP** Briefly describe nature of the material created by this author in which copyright is claimed. ▼

### NOTE

Under the law, the "author" of a "work made for hire" is generally the employer, not the employee (see instructions). For any part of this work that was "made for hire" check "Yes" in the space provided, give the employer (or other person for whom the work was prepared) as "Author" of that part, and leave the space for dates of birth and death blank.

### b

**NAME OF AUTHOR** ▼          **DATES OF BIRTH AND DEATH**
Year Born ▼      Year Died ▼

Was this contribution to the work a "work made for hire"?
☐ Yes
☐ No

**AUTHOR'S NATIONALITY OR DOMICILE**
Name of country
OR { Citizen of ▶_____
Domiciled in ▶_____

**WAS THIS AUTHOR'S CONTRIBUTION TO THE WORK**
Anonymous? ☐ Yes ☐ No
Pseudonymous? ☐ Yes ☐ No
If the answer to either of these questions is "Yes," see detailed instructions.

**NATURE OF AUTHORSHIP** Briefly describe nature of the material created by this author in which copyright is claimed. ▼

### c

**NAME OF AUTHOR** ▼          **DATES OF BIRTH AND DEATH**
Year Born ▼      Year Died ▼

Was this contribution to the work a "work made for hire"?
☐ Yes
☐ No

**AUTHOR'S NATIONALITY OR DOMICILE**
Name of Country
OR { Citizen of ▶_____
Domiciled in ▶_____

**WAS THIS AUTHOR'S CONTRIBUTION TO THE WORK**
Anonymous? ☐ Yes ☐ No
Pseudonymous? ☐ Yes ☐ No
If the answer to either of these questions is "Yes," see detailed instructions.

**NATURE OF AUTHORSHIP** Briefly describe nature of the material created by this author in which copyright is claimed. ▼

## 3

**YEAR IN WHICH CREATION OF THIS WORK WAS COMPLETED** This information must be given in all cases.
◀ Year

**DATE AND NATION OF FIRST PUBLICATION OF THIS PARTICULAR WORK** Complete this information ONLY if this work has been published.
Month ▶_____ Day ▶_____ Year ▶_____
◀ Nation

## 4

See instructions before completing this space.

**COPYRIGHT CLAIMANT(S)** Name and address must be given even if the claimant is the same as the author given in space 2.▼

**TRANSFER** If the claimant(s) named here in space 4 are different from the author(s) named in space 2, give a brief statement of how the claimant(s) obtained ownership of the copyright.▼

APPLICATION RECEIVED

ONE DEPOSIT RECEIVED

TWO DEPOSITS RECEIVED

REMITTANCE NUMBER AND DATE

DO NOT WRITE HERE OFFICE USE ONLY

**MORE ON BACK ▶**
• Complete all applicable spaces (numbers 5-9) on the reverse side of this page.
• See detailed instructions.
• Sign the form at line 8.

DO NOT WRITE HERE

Page 1 of_____pages

**DO NOT WRITE ABOVE THIS LINE. IF YOU NEED MORE SPACE, USE A SEPARATE CONTINUATION SHEET.**

**PREVIOUS REGISTRATION**  Has registration for this work, or for an earlier version of this work, already been made in the Copyright Office?

☐ Yes  ☐ No  If your answer is "Yes," why is another registration being sought? (Check appropriate box) ▼

☐ This is the first published edition of a work previously registered in unpublished form.

☐ This is the first application submitted by this author as copyright claimant.

☐ This is a changed version of the work, as shown by space 6 on this application.

If your answer is "Yes," give: **Previous Registration Number** ▼         **Year of Registration** ▼

**5**

**DERIVATIVE WORK OR COMPILATION**  Complete both space 6a & 6b for a derivative work; complete only 6b for a compilation.

a.  **Preexisting Material**  Identify any preexisting work or works that this work is based on or incorporates. ▼

_____

_____

b.  **Material Added to This Work**  Give a brief, general statement of the material that has been added to this work and in which copyright is claimed. ▼

_____

**6**

See instructions before completing this space.

**DEPOSIT ACCOUNT**  If the registration fee is to be charged to a Deposit Account established in the Copyright Office, give name and number of Account.

Name ▼         Account Number ▼

**7**

**CORRESPONDENCE**  Give name and address to which correspondence about this application should be sent.   Name/Address/Apt/City/State/Zip ▼

_____

_____

_____

Area Code & Telephone Number ▶

Be sure to give your daytime phone ◀ number.

**CERTIFICATION\***  I, the undersigned, hereby certify that I am the

Check only one ▼

☐ author

☐ other copyright claimant

☐ owner of exclusive right(s)

☐ authorized agent of _____
    Name of author or other copyright claimant, or owner of exclusive right(s) ▲

**8**

of the work identified in this application and that the statements made
by me in this application are correct to the best of my knowledge.

**Typed or printed name and date** ▼ If this is a published work, this date must be the same as or later than the date of publication given in space 3.

_____  _date ▶ _____

☞  Handwritten signature (X) ▼

**MAIL
CERTIFI-
CATE TO**

Name ▼

Number/Street/Apartment Number ▼

**Certificate
will be
mailed in
window
envelope**

City/State/ZIP ▼

**Have you:**
● Completed all necessary spaces?
● Signed your application in space 8?
● Enclosed check or money order for $10 payable to *Register of Copyrights?*
● Enclosed your deposit material with the application and fee?

**MAIL TO:** Register of Copyrights, Library of Congress, Washington, D.C. 20559

**9**

# Index

Return of artwork, 29
  in confirmation of assignment,
    22-23
  in contract for receipt and
    holding of artwork, 68
Return of artwork in estimate, 15
Reuse fees, 21
  in book publishing contract, 41
Reversion of rights to author, in
  book publishing contract, 48
Review copies, 46
Revisions, in assignment of work.
    *See also* Assignment of work,
    changes or revisions in
  in book publishing contract, 41,
    46-47
  in collaboration contract, 57
  in confirmation of assignment,
    21-22
  in invoice, 28
Rider, 5
Risk of loss or damage to the work,
  in sale contract, 63
Royalties
  in book publishing contract, 39-45
  on copies of the book sold to
    illustrator, 46
  escalations in rates, 42
  in licensing contract to
    merchandise images, 85-86
  limits on, for tax purposes, 45
  reduced, 42-43
  revisions and, 47
  withholding of, lawsuits and, 45
Rush work, 22, 28

**S**

Sales of artwork. *See also*
    gallery-illustrator contract
    with record of consignment
    and statement of account
  on approval or credit, 74
  contract for, 63-66
  by illustrator, in licensing contract
    to merchandise images, 86
Sales of books, by illustrator, 46
Sales tax, 21, 63
Samples
  in agent-illustrator contract, 34
  in licensing contract to
    merchandise images, 86
Schedule of Artworks, 67
Security interest in artwork
  in contract for receipt and

  holding of artwork, 68
  in gallery-illustrator contract, 75
  gallery-illustrator contract and, 71
  in sale contract, 63, 64
Security interest in a work, 48
*Selling Your Graphic Design and*
  *Illustration,* 11
Sequels, in collaboration contract, 56
Serial rights, 20
  first, 43-44
Shipment of artworks
  in gallery-illustrator contract, 74
  in lecture contract, 82
Signing the contract, 5, 7
Sketches, 14
Sound recordings, in lecture
  contract, 82
Speculation, work on, 22
Standard of care, 23
Standard provisions, 7-10
Statement of account. *See also*
    Accountings
  gallery-illustrator contract with
    record of consignment and, 71-79
Stipend from gallery, 71, 74, 75
Subsidiary rights, in book
  publishing contract, 43, 44, 47
Successors and assigns, 47
  in copyright transfer, 104
  in model release, 90
  in property release, 93
  provision on, 10

**T**

Termination
  agent-illustrator contract, 34, 36
  book publishing contract, 47, 48
  gallery-illustrator contract, 72-73
  licensing contract to merchandise
    images, 86
Term of contract
  agent-illustrator contract, 34
  gallery-illustrator contract, 71, 72
  licensing contract, 85
Theft, in contract for receipt and
  holding of artwork, 68
"Time is of the essence" provision,
  10, 19, 41
Time period of use, in confirmation
  of assignment, 20
Title of book, in book publishing
  contract, 46
Trademarks
  in collaboration contract, 56

  in licensing contract to
    merchandise images, 86
Transfer of copyright, 103-5
Transfer tax, 63
Transportation, in contract for
  receipt and holding of artwork, 68

**U**

Usage rights
  additional, 21
  assignment of, 21

**V**

Value of artwork, 23, 29
Veto power, in book publishing
  contract, 45, 46
Volunteer lawyers for the arts, 10-11

**W**

Waivers
  provision on, 10
  of right to review finished art,
    in property release, 93
    in model release, 90
Warranty and indemnification
  provision, 10
  in agent-illustrator contract, 36
  in book publishing contract,
    39-40, 45
  in collaboration contract, 54, 57
  confirmation of assignment and, 23
Work assignment. *See* Assignment
  of work
Work for hire, 20
Work in progress, submitting
  portions of, 41